M000013615

A Long-Ago Birth in a Right-Now World

A Long-Ago Birth
in a Right-Now World

*Reflections about the Christmas Story
in Our Age and Lives*

Michael B. Brown

WIPF & STOCK · Eugene, Oregon

A LONG-AGO BIRTH IN A RIGHT-NOW WORLD
Reflections about the Christmas Story in Our Age and Lives

Copyright © 2022 Michael B. Brown. All rights reserved. Except for brief quotations in critical publications or reviews, no part of this book may be reproduced in any manner without prior written permission from the publisher. Write: Permissions, Wipf and Stock Publishers, 199 W. 8th Ave., Suite 3, Eugene, OR 97401.

Wipf & Stock
An Imprint of Wipf and Stock Publishers
199 W. 8th Ave., Suite 3
Eugene, OR 97401

www.wipfandstock.com

PAPERBACK ISBN: 978-1-6667-4232-9
HARDCOVER ISBN: 978-1-6667-4233-6
EBOOK ISBN: 978-1-6667-4234-3

Scripture quotations are from the Revised Standard Version of the Bible, copyright © 1946, 1952, and 1971 National Council of the Churches of Christ in the United States of America. Used by permission. All rights reserved worldwide.

CONTENTS

CONTENTS

PREFACE

ADVENT REALLY IS "THE most wonderful time of the year."
Consistently, the world is softer, people are kinder, and the ambiance of life is more cheerful in December than in almost any other month. Even so, those of us who preach, speak, teach, or write sometimes wonder: What's left to say about Christmas? Two thousand years after the event, with millions of sermons having been preached and thousands of books having been written, is it even conceivable that there is anything new or fresh remaining to be said?

Theologically, of course, Christmas is not the pinnacle. That belongs to Easter. Without the resurrection, Jesus would be remembered merely as an effective maverick rabbi who for a while attracted followers but in the end was executed as a political enemy of Rome. In fact, without the resurrection, by this point in time Jesus probably wouldn't be remembered at all. There were countless other popular rabbis in those years whose names have long since been forgotten. His would in all likelihood be among them had it not been for a word from an angel seated atop an empty tomb: "He is not here, for he is risen" (Matt 8:26). That announcement made the story of his life unlike any that of any other from the standpoints of both intrigue and impact. The Christmas part of his life's story is magical. Undeniably, the entire season that has emerged around it is unlike any other time at all.

That being said, let's return to our opening question. Since the Christmas story is so popular, even magical, and is celebrated in an annual festive season called Advent, and since that has been the case for centuries, is there anything new left to be said about it? An obvious answer to the question is "No. It is improbable that any thinker or writer could find a heretofore unexamined idea about the most popular holiday in history." Part of me says "amen" to that. But there is another part of me that isn't so sure. It's not that we haven't heard the Advent message and the Christmas story previously. But for numerous reasons, to *hear* is not always to *listen*. Moments come when the essence of any old, old story can break through to us in a brand new way not because of the tale being retold but because of the listener. Something exists within us at a given moment that didn't exist before. Experiences have shaped us into people who we were not in earlier times. And thus, the new reality of who we are hears a familiar story in ways we weren't prepared to hear formerly.

So, I offer to you a collection of Christmas meditations. Most were originally sermons (though a few were parts of lectures) and, therefore, are based on biblical texts. Some were essays but are still rooted in biblical understandings of the Christmas event. All, I hope, can be appropriated into your personal life in some way that addresses the new you that didn't even exist last December. And even should that not be the case, then perhaps they will at least bring a familiar sense of inner warmth or spiritual challenge that makes this "the most wonderful time of the year."

Michael B. Brown

PART 1

The Writers

THEY WERE DIFFERENT MEN addressing different audiences under different circumstances. Thus, we should not expect the way they constructed their stories to be identical. In fact, sometimes those stories are not even similar.

Mark was the first of the Gospel writers, composing his book sometime around 60–65 CE. He wrote prior to the Jewish uprising against Rome in 70 CE that was unsuccessful in heartbreaking and devastating ways. When Mark did his writing, the Jews were experiencing oppression from Nero, and the movement called "Christianity" (still looked upon by many simply to be a sect of Judaism) was experiencing outright persecution. Mark's target audience was the latter group. He wrote in a difficult and uncertain age. His readers were on the receiving end of accusations and abuse. A central message from Mark to people in that particular boat was not to give up the ship. Someone had come who would soon come again, and he had greater power than did the emperor of Rome.

Luke wrote a decade or more after Mark and, just as Matthew also would do, used a good portion of the first Gospel as a blueprint for constructing his own. However, whereas Mark had written primarily to an audience of people who had already joined The Church, Luke wrote to people who were merely thinking about it. A physician from the city of Rome and a traveler with Paul, the

1

great evangelist, Luke targeted not so much the people in the boat as those on the shore watching it sail. He wrote to people who had not yet boarded the vessel to begin a life-transforming journey but who were slowly inching their way toward the dock while giving the journey serious thought. Mark's readers already knew the story (including the details of both the birth and resurrection accounts). Luke's, on the other hand, were outsiders and (what we would call) "seekers." So, while Mark could get away with addressing merely what Jesus did and would do again, Luke had to become more of an educator. His first job was to inform people who Jesus was (to be biographical), providing intricate accounts of what Mark's readers already knew by heart. Mark began with the ministry of Christ. Luke had to go all the way back and set the stage in order for his gentile readers to know who and what he was writing about when the ministry stories began. At the heart of his mission was the goal of convincing readers who felt like outliers that the Messiah was inclusive and cared just as much about them as he did about Jewish Christians. There was room for Romans and other gentiles in the boat.

Matthew's Gospel is the third of the written narratives about the life of Jesus, probably composed between 75 and 85 CE. Like Luke, he wrote after the fall of Jerusalem. Unlike Luke, that event was a more pressing issue for Matthew. Why? Because his target audience was neither Christians nor seekers but Jews. Matthew was a Jewish Christian writing to Jewish readers about the Jewish Messiah. The most famous section of his book is the Sermon on the Mount (chapters 5–7). Unlike Luke, where Jesus delivers the sermon on the plain standing beside the waters, Matthew makes certain to have Jesus ascend to the top of a hill, much as Moses ascended Mount Sinai. Once there, "when he sat down his disciples came to him. And he opened his mouth and taught them" (Matt 5:1–2). That way of teaching is called the "rabbinic method." When a rabbi walked with his disciples (a word which means "students"), there would be dialogue—questions, answers, exchanges of ideas, and responses often through a rabbinic literary device called "midrash." But when the rabbi sat down, his students knew the time for dialogue had ended. They had moved from conversation to education. Now he would teach, and they would listen. So Matthew constructed his most famous story in a fashion every Jewish reader would understand. And what was the corpus of those three chapters? The Sermon on the Mount is simply and solely a reinterpretation of the law of Moses: "You have heard that it was said . . . [then came words from Moses], but I say unto you . . . [then came words from Jesus interpreting the former words]" (e.g., Matt 5:21, 27, 31, 33, 38, 43). Only Matthew has Jesus making this statement: "Think not that I have come to abolish the law and the prophets; I have come not to abolish them but to fulfil them" (Matt 5:17). Only in the context of historic Judaism can we understand Matthew's version of the birth story—a version including a variety of Moses imagery and also including a genealogy that connected Jesus to Abraham and David (and did so through Joseph, as opposed to Luke's focus on Mary). To people who had fallen to oppressors from Rome, Matthew wrote with empathy and hope, reminding them that their long-awaited Messiah had, in fact, come. And if they cast their lots with him, his power was greater than that of Nero, Vespasian, Titus, or any other emperor or tyrant who would seek to defeat them.

John's is the Fourth Gospel, composed as little as ten or as much as twenty-five years following Matthew's. John, like his predecessors, wrote in a unique style crafted for a particular audience. Not first-century Christians. Not Roman outliers. Not Jews reeling from a recent military downfall. John wrote primarily to Greek readers, people who cut their teeth on the philosophical compositions of Socrates, Plato, and Aristotle, people who were first and foremost thinkers and seekers of ultimate truth. They did not find the tales of angels' songs and shepherds and innkeepers and mangers and wise men as compelling as did those who read Luke or Matthew. John's readers were instead intrigued by ideas and their sources. Thus, he began his Gospel in a very different way when explaining who Jesus was and how he got here: "In the beginning was the Word [*Logos*]," he wrote (John 1:1), using a word that means "mind" or "thought." People of faith employ versions of that word all the time. "Theology," for example, is a blending of the Greek words *Theos* (God) and *Logos* (mind), basically meaning "thought about God." "Christology" blends *Christ* and *Logos*, thus meaning "thought about Christ." So, John began his Gospel to Greek thinkers by saying, "In the beginning was *the mind of God* . . . and the mind of God became flesh and dwelt among us, full of grace and *Truth*" (my translation of John 1:1, 14, italics added). John and Mark shared a common opinion that what mattered most was not how Jesus got here. Where they took somewhat different roads afterward is that Mark concentrated on what Jesus did once he was here (his actions), while John concentrated on what Jesus represented to discerning minds (his essence).

The mere reading of Advent/Christmas devotional literature can inform, comfort, and inspire. But to plumb the depths of what is read, a person needs at least some modest acquaintance with the author of that text and his audience, outlook, and intent. As I often tell my undergrad biblical-studies students: "Every text must be read in context." Hopefully, this brief account of who did the ancient writings will help illumine the divine subject they wrote about.

MARK WITH NO MANGER

Ushered into the banker's office, I took a seat on the other side of his oversized mahogany desk, smiled, and said, "Thank you so much for seeing me. My goodness, you have a beautiful office." He replied, "How much do you need, and why do you need it?" Clearly, he was a cut-to-the-chase kind of guy. It was obvious to him that his directness took me a bit off guard, so he explained. "I don't mean to be rude, but I go to my club for chitchat. I come here for business. My business is to make loans, as long as they seem justified. So, let's get down to brass tacks. How much do you need, and why do you need it?"

Mark was that sort of guy. His is the First Gospel, written ten to fifteen years before Luke's, that many or more before Matthew's, and perhaps as much as forty years before John's. Whereas each of the other three writers tell a version of the Christmas story (Matthew and Luke in particular detail), Mark skips right past that. No angels, no shepherds, no wise men from the east, no inn, no manger, no virgin mother or confused dad threatening to put her away silently. Mark gets down to brass tacks by beginning the story of Christ with the statement: "Now after John was arrested, Jesus came into Galilee, preaching the gospel of God, and saying, 'The time is fulfilled, and the kingdom of God is at hand; repent, and believe in the gospel'" (Mark 1:14–15).

Why did Mark write as he did? Unlike the other three Gospel authors, Mark was writing primarily to people who had been there, people who were already Christian converts and, therefore, knew the details of the Jesus story. Mark didn't have to remind them of the birth, just as he didn't include any post-resurrection appearances of Christ either. They already knew the miracles at the beginning and the end of the story. Mark wrote to tell them the importance of what happened in between those stories. In fact, he apparently felt it was not the birth of Jesus that mattered but the life—not how he got here but what he accomplished once he did.

Mark felt the messianic nature of Christ was best illustrated not necessarily by a miraculous birth beneath a star in a manger but instead by the concrete actions of cleansing lepers, or opening the eyes of the blind, or giving a paralytic the ability to stand, take up his pallet, and walk.

Mark believed Jesus' essence was also revealed in his unwavering commitments. Even late in the game, both family and close friends encouraged him to return to Capernaum and lie low until the heat was off. But Jesus would not be distracted from his mission, however dangerous it was. Luke (who used Mark as one of his primary sources when writing his own Gospel) says, "He set his face to go to Jerusalem" (Luke 9:51). He made an irreversible decision that no one could talk him out of. Once there, he told his disciples, "Greater love has no man than this, that a man lay down his life for his friends" (John 15:13).

Specific actions born of sacred commitments—that is where Mark believed Jesus' messianic role was most clearly evident. It was not in his birth but in his life that Mark said we see the Messiah come to earth: in his love for children, the poor, the sick, the outcasts, the oppressed, the sinful, the rejected, the victimized, and the vulnerable. Matthew (who included about two-thirds of Mark's Gospel in his own) quotes Jesus as saying, "Come to me, all who labor and are heavy laden, and I will give you rest" (Matt 11:28). In his life and his love, his lordship is revealed.

Mark was particularly concerned with members of the infant Church who were experiencing persecution under Caesar Nero.

Storms were brewing in the empire. In those days, the church was symbolized by the image of a boat. Thus, Mark included stories of storms at sea, the boat being rocked to and fro, and the sailors being pummeled and frightened, but Jesus was always present in or near or coming toward the boat with power to calm the seas.

A lady I know taught a children's Sunday school class in a small church for half a century. She had a million stories of kids she knew across those years—ones with promise who failed to live up to their potential and ones who didn't reveal much potential as youngsters but went on to have unparalleled success. She told stories of sweet children, mischievous children, funny children, and the sometimes tender and sometimes off-the-wall things they said or did.

One story she loved to tell in December was about Mary Lynn, a little girl with Down syndrome. The other children were usually kind to Mary Lynn, but sometimes children will be children and, as such, will show off at someone else's expense. Sadly, Mary Lynn was often the target. On the Sunday after Christmas, the teacher went around the room asking every child one by one what Santa had left under the tree. Each little girl and boy was so anxious to report that they could barely wait for the preceding one to finish. "I got a bike, a book, a video game, a new dress, a baseball glove . . . ," and on and on the stories went until the teacher reached Mary Lynn. "What did Santa bring you?" she asked, and the child, in her somewhat slow and halting style of speech, answered, "A birthday cake."

The other children erupted with laughter. "We didn't ask what you got for you birthday, Mary Lynn!" "It's not your birthday, Mary Lynn!" "She asked you about Santa, Mary Lynn!"

Defiantly, and fighting back tears, the child answered, "I got a cake for Jesus' birthday." The teacher understood. Mary Lynn came from a poor home where gifts and Santa were out of the question. Apparently, her mother had told the child that Christmas isn't about gifts and Santa but about Jesus—about what he did for us and how he loves us and how he takes care of all his children. And thus, knowing how good and kind he is, we need to wish him a happy birthday. It is likely that the mother had gone to the day-old bakery, where grocery stores return breads and cakes that are past their expiration dates and can be sold at a discount. A piece of almost-too-old cake and a tiny candle were all they could afford . . . that and the message that the special day was not about trees, reindeer, and gifts (as enjoyable as those things are) but actually about Jesus. And it was not just about his birth, Mary Lynn had likely been told, but more especially about what came next—his love and his life and how that gives hope to all the little Mary Lynns in the world. The retired teacher used to tell that story and say, "I look back across the years and think of her and how she, of all the children I ever taught, probably understood Christmas best of all."

Mark got that. Christmas was about Jesus—not just how he was born, but why *and* what he did once he got here. It's about what happened when he grew up, who he became, all that he stood for, all that he offered the world, and all that he still offers to each of us. The very first Gospel ever written does not begin with a manger. Instead, it begins with a ministry. It begins by saying, "Now after John was arrested, Jesus came into Galilee, preaching the gospel of God, and saying, 'The time is fulfilled, and the kingdom of God is at hand; repent, and believe in the gospel'" (Mark 1:14–15).

2

LUKE'S MESSIAH
FOR ONE AND ALL

"In those days a decree went out from Caesar Augustus that all the world should be enrolled" (Luke 2:1). So begins the most treasured of all the Christmas stories. It was written toward the end of the first century for outsiders, for gentiles and Romans, for folks who had never been identified as and had never felt like "God's chosen people." His Gospel begins with a greeting: "It seemed good to me also, having followed all things closely for some time past, to write an orderly account for you, most excellent The-oph'ilus" (Luke 1:3). Who was he addressing? Opinions vary about that. Some think Theophilus was an individual, perhaps an official in the court of the Caesar. Others believe the word may simply have been the blending of two Greek words, *theos* and *philos*, which translates as "those who think about God." If the latter is true, Luke may have been writing to a gentile audience whom we would call "religious seekers." He wrote to a nontraditional audience—to Romans, Greeks, and gentiles—about a newborn Messiah who came for all and not just for some.

In a crowded New Jersey mall in mid-December, a social worker led a group of children through the line to see Santa. They were children who had next to nothing and, in fact, had no one. Residents of a state home, Christmas by Christmas they received meager gifts: some fruit, a coloring book, a picture puzzle, and not much more. One at a time, they climbed onto Santa's lap and shared dreams of what they wanted but in all likelihood would never find beneath a tree. Then came one child, a little boy maybe eight or nine years old. When Santa asked, "What would you like this year?" his answer was not "a baseball glove," "a bicycle," or "a remote-controlled car." Instead, he replied, "I want a family." Santa knew that couples traditionally desire to adopt infants and that the older children get, the less likely it is that anyone will invite them home. What was that shopping-mall Santa to say as he held a little boy on his lap and the child's heart in his hands? Pointing to a nearby manger scene, he said, "See that baby over there?" The child nodded. Santa continued, "You're part of his family already. He came all the way from heaven just to choose you." There followed a moment of predictable chat, after which the child left, never to be seen again by that Christmas worker. Maybe he got his wish and some mom and dad took him into their home to nurture and love him. Maybe he didn't. But either way, what he was told that day on Santa's lap was true: "For to you is born this day in the city of David a Savior" (Luke 2:11) who came to make everyone part of his family.

The rich and powerful (like Caesar) . . . the poor and forgotten (like the shepherds or that orphaned child in a mall) . . . the lonely or left out (like all the Marys and Josephs of our world) . . . the grieving, the tired, the aged, the frightened, the guilty . . . He comes and calls all of them—and all of us— "family." So said Luke in the most famous Christmas story ever written: "For to *all* is born this day a Savior." He makes room for everyone at the manger.

When I was pastor of Marble Collegiate Church in New York City, there was a man who sat daily on the steps of our church on Fifth Avenue. He was an aging African American gentleman in worn clothes, an amputee with one pant leg pinned up at the knee, always wearing the same US Army baseball cap and always carrying two paper cups (one for the coffee he would get from the church kitchen and another for coins that passersby might choose to drop into it). Early morning or late afternoon, in summer's heat or winter's cold, you were likely to find him there, always with a ready smile and the words "I hope you're having the best day ever!" On one of those days, which decidedly had not been the best ever, I exited my office, rounded the corner to head to the subway, and once again saw him. Usually, I smiled, spoke, and walked on by. But that day, for whatever reason, I spoke and stopped walking. He provided his usual greeting, and I answered, "The best day ever? Not really. This day has been alright—some good things, some not so good."

"But you keep showing up," he said with his unfailing smile. "So you must hope every day that something good is going to happen in there."

I nodded, aware that on most days, countless wonderful things did, in fact, happen in there. "Why do you keep showing up?" I asked him.

"I keep showing up here," he said, "because this is a spot where I feel safe and I feel noticed. I don't know how to say it exactly, but when I get here it's like I'm part of something. I have a place that says 'stay' instead of 'go.'"

The Christmas story, as Luke tells it, is about folks who have been made to feel like outliers. But suddenly, a star appears, and angels sing, and those who were on the outside "feel connected to something." And that something is, in fact, someone who calls them (and us) "family": "For to you is born this day in the city of David a Savior, who is Christ the Lord" (Luke 2:11).

3

MATTHEW'S CHRISTMAS AUDIENCE

Matthew wrote his Gospel primarily to Hebrew readers, which is why he included some things that are a bit different from the other Gospels. Matthew was essentially a Jewish Christian writing to a Jewish audience about the birth of a Jewish Messiah.

The theological predispositions of his readers explain why he began his Gospel with a lengthy genealogy: "Abraham was the father of Isaac, and Isaac the father of Jacob, and Jacob the father of Judah and his brothers . . ." And on and on it goes until we read, "And Jesse the father of David the king. And David was the father of Solomon . . ." And still on and on it goes until at last we read, "And Jacob the father of Joseph the husband of Mary, of whom Jesus was born, who is called Christ" (see Matt 1:1–16).

Why did Matthew start with that long (and, we sometimes think, boring) list of forty-two generations from Abraham to Jesus? Because every faithful Jew in his targeted audience had been taught from childhood that the Messiah had to be a descendant of Abraham and David. Without those connections, let the person walk on water, heal the sick, raise the dead, or be raised himself— none of that would be enough, in their minds, for him to be the Messiah (God's chosen one). The Messiah had to be a descendant of Abraham and David; no exceptions.

Edward VIII was the king of England for one year. His was not only a brief but a decidedly inglorious season for the monarchy. He disdained many of the customs associated with being king and offended traditionalists by wanting to do away with those customs. Strike one. He denied royal protocol by proposing marriage to a twice-divorced American woman who was not part of British aristocracy. As titular head of the Church of England, that was not allowed. That was enough to cause many leaders of Parliament to threaten to resign. Strike two. As if all of that were not sufficient, there were even strong suspicions that Edward (and his new bride) were Nazi sympathizers. Big strike three! After one year, he resigned, and England breathed a sigh of relief. In truth, there were countless people in England at that point in time who would have been far more capable monarchs—including Prime Minister Baldwin and soon-to-be Prime Minister Churchill. But, abilities notwithstanding, it was bloodline that mattered. Baldwin and Churchill were not descendants of the ancient kings and queens. So, whatever talents they may have possessed, they did not possess the one requirement that was nonnegotiable. Being king was ultimately an inherited virtue.[1]

Jesus had greater gifts and powers than anyone else who had ever lived. But had he not been in the bloodline of Abraham and David, no faithful Hebrew would have proclaimed him "king." Joseph, Jesus' father, was in that bloodline, which is why Matthew began his Gospel with the genealogy.

By now, however, some of you are thinking, "Wait a minute! There's a flaw in that argument. Joseph wasn't Jesus' daddy. Not really. Mary was a virgin when she gave birth. Jesus was 'conceived of the Holy Spirit.' So, what difference does it make whether or not Joseph was a descendant of Abraham or David or anybody else?" Here's why it matters. At that time in Jewish culture, the male who named a child was legally considered the child's father. He could be an uncle, a granddad, a neighbor, or a friend. But the male who named the baby was immediately considered the "parent." So,

1. For more information, see Van der Kiste, "King Edward VIII"; and Parris, "Edward VIII's Abdication."

that's why Matthew had the angel instruct Joseph, not Mary, to name the baby. "[Mary] will bear a son," the angel said to Joseph, "and *you* shall call his name Jesus" (Matt 1:20–21, italics added). Once Joseph named the baby, he was immediately accepted as Jesus' father, and therefore, from that moment Jesus was considered a descendant of Abraham and David—the "son of Abraham." "Jesus, Son of David . . . !" they called him (Luke 18:38). With those words, Matthew's readers were willing to entertain the idea that Jesus could be their Messiah, their King.

So, what's our takeaway from all this? Consider three brief things.

First, Matthew's elevation of Joseph's status reminds us that even those who are often overlooked are still valuable contributors. Not only the pilot of the jet but also the worker who secured the bolts that kept the wings in place; not only the high school basketball coach but also the custodian who kept the gym floor clean and polished; not only the surgeon but also the operating-room technician who made sure all the instruments were on the tray; not only the sculptor but also the quarrier who dug the stones—all are absolutely indispensable. By reminding us of the importance of Joseph, Matthew reminds us that all persons, even those too often overlooked or ignored, are vital and valued.

Second, Matthew wrote in a specific way to a specific audience, reminding us that God speaks to us where we are. The journey of faith is like riding a train. We don't all have to be in the same car. We are simply all moving in the same direction. We don't all have to know the Bible' stories equally, or understand theology similarly, or interpret things uniformly. God loves each of us as we are. Whatever car of the train we occupy, God will find us there.

Third, as is the case in all the Gospels, Matthew's story is ultimately about Jesus. Luke emphasizes Mary's lineage, but in the end it's about the birth of Jesus, not about his mom. Matthew emphasizes Joseph's lineage, but in the end it's about the birth of Jesus, not about his dad. John summed it up for both Matthew and Luke when he wrote, "And the Word became flesh and dwelt among us, full of grace and truth" (John 1:14).

The early Puritans refused to celebrate Christmas Day. Even into the mid-1800s in as progressive a city as Boston, children went to school on Christmas Day. Trees, lights, gifts, and Santa were not allowed. Why? Because they contended that if we celebrate the birth of Christ only one day a year, we have missed its meaning. Instead, it should be celebrated every day throughout the year. Every day should be an observance of prayer and piety, worship and works, devotion and dedication to him.[2] Those Puritans believed that is what the Bible teaches—that in the final tally, Christmas really is all about Jesus. That's why we hear so often the phrase "Let's keep Christ in Christmas." This doesn't mean that we should give up any of the fun and festive things we do in December. Those things continue to remind us of the arrival of Jesus and how earth-changing that was. Instead, hopefully, we simply remember why we do those fun and festive things. Thanks to Matthew, we are reminded that Christmas is *for* everyone but is *about* Jesus.

2. See Tourgee, "Puritans Banned Christmas."

4

JOHN'S LIGHT IN THE DARKNESS

Throughout the ages, both in literature and music, images of light and darkness have been the basis of many a tale. We read of a character "sinking in dark despair." We sing "Walking on Sunshine," "You Are the Sunshine of My Life," or (for those of us of a certain age) "Let the Sunshine In."[1] How many a poem or soliloquy has begun with the words "From the dawn of creation," and how many a good thriller has begun with the words "It was a dark and stormy night"?

John begins his Gospel by employing those images. Unlike Matthew and Luke, John wrote to a primarily Greek audience that was not so much interested in biography as in theology. They didn't ask as much about the traditional birth story as they asked, "What is the significance of that story to us?" The contrast of light and darkness was a well-known Socratic theme to his Greek readers. Socrates compared us to people who gaze into dim caves and think that the shadows we see dancing on the walls are reality. Instead, said Socrates, reality is in the world

---

1. By Katrina and the Waves, Stevie Wonder, and James Rado, Gerome Ragni, and Galt MacDermot, respectively.

of light behind us. Truth is found only when someone turns us toward that light, enabling us at last to see what exists there.[2]

"And the Word became flesh and dwelt among us," says John (John 1:14). "The light shines in the darkness, and the darkness has not overcome it" (John 1:5). John's audience would have grasped that concept immediately—the concept that God had entered the world and turned us around so that we would no longer peer into the shadows but instead would be filled with light and with the truth, comfort, and grace that it reveals.

A former church member of mine lost two daughters in a traffic accident and came very close to losing a son in a separate incident. For several years, that mother went through a deep depression born of grief, trying everything she could but not being able to regain her emotional equilibrium. When at last a "new normal" did come for her (with a sense of resolution and peace), she described to me her years of despair. She said, "It was like being in a long tunnel. You know there used to be daylight before you entered it, and you believe that there is still daylight somewhere on the other side. But every turn you take just leads deeper into a tunnel where there is nothing but darkness."

We also know about the darkness, don't we?

- Sitting in an ICU waiting room late at night . . .
- Driving home in the rain after losing a job . . .
- Lying awake as a parent, worried about your child on the highway or in a war zone on the other side of the world . . .
- Locking the door for the last time after your business failed . . .
- Hearing the diagnosis: cancer or Alzheimer's . . .
- Staying in love even though the other person no longer feels the same.

2. See Rheins, "Plato's Allegory."

If we know about darkness, then John's is a word we need to hear and claim as our own: "And the Word became flesh and dwelt among us" in the midst of our pain (John 1:14); and when that Word takes up residence at our sides, says John, "the light shines in the darkness, and the darkness has not overcome it" (John 1:5). In any season of stress or sadness, he comes to us, to be with us and for us, to hold us up when otherwise we would fall. This one who later calls himself "the light of the world" dispels our shadows (John 8:12).

A long time ago, I heard a preacher tell the following story: When she was two years old, a child from Philadelphia named Carrie was involved in an automobile accident, suffering a serious head injury that resulted in total loss of vision. Until age fourteen, she was completely blind. Then she underwent successful surgery at the Hospital of the University of Pennsylvania. Full vision was restored in one eye, and partial vision in another.

Carrie told of the morning when the bandages were removed and how at first there was the startling presence of light. When her eyes began to adjust, she saw two faces. One was the face of her doctor. The other was the face of a woman with tears of love on her cheeks who kept whispering, "Carrie. Carrie."

"I knew," said the young woman, "that she was my mother. Her face was attached to the voice that had called my name those twelve years in the darkness."

"The Word became flesh and dwelt among us." Jesus came to live where we live and to call our names in the darkness.

"A Light has shined in the darkness, and the darkness cannot overcome it." John says that Jesus, who was born to be with us in the shadows, will also, in time, remove the bandages and turn the lights back on in our lives. The pain and fears that grasp us now will vanish then. And when that occurs, hope, happiness, and wholeness will be restored.

That is the Christmas story as John told it.

PART 2

The Message

ACCORDING TO BOTH LUKE and Matthew, the story of the arrival of the Messiah begins with angel visitations. An angel appears to Zechariah. An angel appears to Mary. An angel appears (and then reappears) to Joseph. An angel, backed up by a celestial choir, appears to shepherds on a hillside outside Bethlehem. On each occasion, the mere mortals in the story are initially gripped by fear (and understandably so). Therefore, each time the angel has to calm them down a bit before imparting "good news of a great joy" (Luke 2:10).

That good news, of course, is that one will enter the human realm where heartache and hope, hurt and humor, hard times and happiness all coexist. His coming will make sense of things for those who, as Isaiah put it, "[walk] in darkness" but hang onto a faith that "on them has light shined" (Isa 9:2).

So, who is this one who came and who, in our right-now world of Advent, we pray will come again? What was his nature? What were his teachings? What difference does his arrival make in our lives if we open ourselves up to it? What does he demand? And what does he promise? Those questions lie at the heart of the Christmas message . . . the long-ago message . . . the contemporary message . . . the message for shepherds, a carpenter, and his betrothed . . . and the message for you and me.

5

CHRISTOLOGY

Christology is "the study of Christ," a systematized effort to define his nature and attributes. Our ancient Jewish forebears did not make that effort as complicated as we tend to do. In Hebrew Scripture, messianic prophecies almost always boiled down to God's sending someone who would "deliver" the people of Israel via military leadership and power. In fact, when you access any source providing a definition of the word "messiah," in addition to "chosen" and "anointed," you are certain to see the word "deliverer." Micah, Jeremiah, Isaiah—pick your prophet. They all prayed for and dreamed of a Messiah who would deliver God's chosen people from their oppressors.

More than once, Jesus was referred to as "thou, Son of David" by people (often Zealots) who hoped for a deliverer who would reestablish the throne of Israel with all the pomp and power reported from the Davidic era. When Jesus entered Jerusalem on the first Palm Sunday, the crowds shouted, "Hosanna!" We interpret that word to mean "welcome." It actually meant "Save us now!" In other words, "Be the Messiah we have longed for, thou, Son of David." Many scholars suspect that Judas ultimately betrayed Jesus because, as a Zealot, Judas wanted a military Messiah and Jesus was not acting like one. So, their conjecture is that Judas put Jesus in a position where he would be forced to do what every Zealot assumed the Messiah was intended (and had inherent power) to do.

What Judas learned too late—and the other Zealots in time came to learn—was that Jesus was a different kind of Messiah from what they had expected. "My kingship is not of this world" (John 18:36), he said, contrary to their expectations. He didn't come to change the world; he came to change us. That does not mean, of course, that his followers are freed from a sense of moral responsibility. It certainly does not mean that we should remain silent or inactive in light of political atrocities or human oppression. But it does mean that the Messiah came to transform lives more than to restore a Davidic political order. Be in the world but not of it (see John 17:14). Still very much a deliverer, the Messiah simply delivers us in ways unimagined in Zealots' dreams.

A New Testament word for "salvation" is *metanoia*. Think of metamorphosis, the changing of one thing into something different and lovelier (like the caterpillar that becomes a butterfly). That, said Jesus, is what the Messiah came to initiate—not a new political kingdom but a new personal one where an individual is sufficiently transformed that it's almost as if he or she were "born again," given the chance to start over (John 3:3).

Years ago at a meeting of a Guideposts advisory committee, a man and his wife shared his story with my wife and me. That story was of a man who (in his words) "had lived a decent life—not bad or evil, but not all that happy or meaningful, either. Most things in my life tended to be either a struggle or a bore. There was no joy." His wife, a more deeply spiritual person than he, more or less forced him to accompany her to a movie she wanted to see. It was showing at the church she attended (almost always alone). The film was about the life of the famous evangelist E. Stanley Jones. There was a moment in the movie when God spoke to Jones. The man telling us the story said, "In that moment, it was no longer a movie. I heard God's voice speaking to me, calling me, encouraging me. And while everyone was simply watching a film, I prayed in silence and poured out my frustrations, fears, and failings. I remember at one point saying, 'God, life is too hard. It's wearing me out. If you're willing, I wish you would take it over for me.' From that moment I could feel a change begin, a shift toward energy, vision, happiness, and hope." He looked at us, virtually beaming with happiness as he told his story, and said, "I went in to see a movie as one person and came out as a different one." His wife chuckled and added, "And I like the new person so much better!"

Metanoia. It's one of the key things the Messiah accomplishes *for* and *in* people when he arrives. He transforms the old into the new, like a caterpillar into a butterfly. He helps purge detrimental characteristics that get in the way of abundant living: greed, guilt, hatred, hostility, bias, bigotry, fear, fatalism, anger, apathy, self-doubt, sin. Those things are deleted and replaced by other things like happiness, wholeness, and hope. Biblical Christology describes a Messiah who comes not to overthrow Herod and Caesar but instead to shift our loyalties to a greater kingdom of truth, kindness, and civility. If we allow him to do his designed work, then whatever the world around us is like, we become new creatures who experience the realities of peace and meaning.

In truth, when the Messiah arrives, he simply restores us to what and who we were originally designed to be. That, too, is *metanoia*—not so much a movement toward that which is new and unheard of but instead a movement toward that which is new but also originally intended. The purpose of the little creature from the outset was not to be a caterpillar but rather to be a butterfly.

An acquaintance related to me the story of something that occurred in California, his home state. Apparently, it had made some of the local newspapers, mostly buried away on some back page where the paper needed something merely to serve as "filler." Those who stopped reading at the headlines, sports section, or editorials missed the most important story of that day. It was about a nine-year-old boy who was playing baseball with other kids from a housing development. A playground outside his third-story apartment served as the ball field. The little boy was not particularly good at catching the ball. Ordinarily, baseballs hit his way would go through his legs or past his outstretched glove, or they bounced off his arms. So, his friends put him in right field, where he was least likely to have to catch anything at all.

One afternoon during a game, he glanced up at the windows of his apartment and saw his two-year-old sister standing on the kitchen table watching the big kids play ball outside. She was leaning against the window screen, and it was bulging outward. Her brother began to yell at her, "Get back! Get back! Don't push on the window." But she either failed to hear or failed to understand, being so caught up in her longing to be downstairs playing with the older children. Her brother watched in horror as the screen broke free and his little sister fell from the window and rapidly descended toward the ground three stories below. The brother stationed himself, held out his arms, and miraculously caught her, the two of them tumbling to the ground together and managing to do so without injury.

Word of that event spread rather quickly through the apartment complex. A local news reporter heard about the incident and decided to interview the nine-year-old child. The reporter asked the little boy, "How did you feel as you prepared to catch your sister?" He answered, "Pretty scared, 'cause I ain't too good at catchin'!" But catch he did. He broke her fall, protected her from serious injury or even death, took her hand, and led her back up to where she was meant to be.

The friend who told me about it said, "When I read that story back on page 8 or 9 of section C, I remember thinking that there's something about it that makes me think of Jesus."

He was correct. The one who comes at Christmas positions himself to catch us when we fall, to pick us up and carry us back to where we were meant to be. And once we get there, by his grace and power we are made new. A butterfly exists where before there was a caterpillar. That quality, the power to transform, is part of our understanding of Christology—who Jesus is and what he does in and for us.

6

BE CAREFUL WHAT YOU ASK FOR

I have received some strange requests over my years in ministry. All clergy do. Once a groom asked if his dog could serve as the best man in his wedding. Another time, I was requested to perform baptisms in a backyard swimming pool. You wouldn't believe some of the things I have been asked to eat at potluck dinners. "Taste this, Reverend. I killed, cleaned, and cooked it myself!"

One of the most unusual things anyone ever asked me to do was when I officiated at a memorial service at a funeral home in Asheville, North Carolina. The daughter of the deceased gentleman requested that during the service I sing "Amazing Grace." Clearly, she had never heard me sing. What she asked for would be like requesting the Aflac Duck to sing—maybe worse. But she asked, so I did it . . . sort of. I invited the attendees to sing along with me. To their everlasting credit, by midway through the first verse, the congregation began to sing the hymn with sufficient volume to effectively drown me out. Following the service, I received two comments that have stuck with me ever since. One was from the funeral director, who said, "That will teach her to be careful what she's asking for!" The other was from a member of my congregation who simply observed, "Wow! That woman must have really hated her father!"

"Be careful what you ask for." For centuries, the people of Israel asked for a Messiah. They prayed that God would send a "chosen one" to live with them and deliver them from their enemies, and they were quick to describe what they assumed the Messiah would be like once he arrived. He would possess political power and military strength and would shower favor on some people over against other people whom they disdained. He would be Davidic in his capacities as a ruler and mighty in his reign. In Isaiah's words:

> For the yoke of his burden,
>   and the staff for his shoulder,
>   the rod of his oppressor,
>   thou hast broken as on the day of Mid'ian.
>   . . .
> For to us a child is born,
>   to us a son is given;[1]
> and the government will be upon his shoulder,
>   and his name will be called
> "Wonderful Counselor,[2] Mighty God,[3]
>   Everlasting Father,[4] Prince of Peace."[5]
> Of the increase of his government and of peace
>   there will be no end,
> upon the throne of David, and over his kingdom
>   . . . (Isa 9:4–7)

That's what they asked for: might, power, strength, military dominance, a politician, a general, a sword and shield—"Of the increase of his government . . there will be no end, upon the throne of David . . ."

---

1. As in "Son of David."
2. A reference to King Solomon.
3. A source of limitless power.
4. A reference to Abraham.
5. A political Messiah.

26

They asked for a Messiah, and God sent one. But be careful what you ask for, because the Messiah God sent and the one Isaiah described were not at all the same. Might, power, strength, military dominance? "And she gave birth to her first-born son and wrapped him in swaddling cloths, and laid him in a manger, because there was no place for them in the inn" (Luke 2:7). Throughout his life, far from establishing a military kingdom, he preached a gospel of mercy and reconciliation: "Love your enemies and pray for those who persecute you" (Matt 5:44). At last, only hours before being led away not to be crowned as a political sovereign but to be executed as a political prisoner, he reiterated the central theme of his whole life: "This is my commandment, that you love one another . . ." (John 15:12). Even while dying on the cross, he demonstrated what that looks like when he prayed for the very people who had driven the spikes through his flesh and said, "Father, forgive them . . ." (Luke 23:34).

Be careful what you ask for when praying the Christmas prayer *Maranatha* ("Lord, come!"), because when he comes, it is as a messenger of love, and love demands more of us than might or power ever could.

A friend of many years told me of attending her son's kindergarten Christmas pageant when he was five years old (he's now thirty-five). The children did skits, sang songs, and recited one-verse poems. Parents and grandparents smiled broadly and applauded enthusiastically at each offering along the way. At one point, the children were handed large cardboard letters to hold over their heads, spelling out the title of the song they were about to sing, a song called "Christmas Love." Thirteen children stood there, each holding a cardboard letter that would be held up one at a time as the song progressed. When a verse said, "*C* is for 'Christmas,'" the first child in line held up the letter *C*. When the next verse said, "*H* is for 'happy,'" that child held up the *H*. On and on it went, slowly spelling out the title "Christmas Love" until they came to the little girl with the letter *M*. When she lifted her piece of cardboard over her head, she was holding it upside down. So, rather than seeing an *M*, the audience saw the letter *W* instead. A couple kids noticed and snickered. Most parents smiled and thought of it as one of the cute things you expect at pageants like those. At the conclusion of the song, however, the snickering ended and the smiles changed into a hushed awareness of what had been accidentally communicated. By inverting the *M* into a *W*, the message no longer said "Christmas Love." Instead, all those gathered in the school cafeteria saw a different message: "Christ was love."

And so he was, and so he still is. The Messiah came to the world and still comes to us as God's gift of love. Pure and simple. People of faith seem to understand that intuitively. And so, in December we sing of how love came down at Christmas. We teach our children "Jesus loves me, this I know." We hang ornaments on our trees with hand-painted words: "The greatest of these is love" (1 Cor 13:13).

"And this will be a sign for you," the angels sang over Bethlehem (Luke 2:12), and that sign pointed toward the primacy of love. That's why Jesus came—to set unbridled, unconditional, unending love into motion. The Messiah who comes asks us to keep that force moving forward, to be his conduits through which the divine gift remains alive. In the home, in the workplace, in the neighborhood, in the church, in a fractured culture so clearly dominated by anger and partisanship, in all our relationships, he calls us to practice kindness, to offer forgiveness, to extend charity, to believe the best about people, and to show our best to people: "This is my commandment, that you love one another . . ." (John 15:12). Be careful what you ask for, because if you ask for a Messiah, that is what you will receive. And love is what he will ask of you.

7

MYSTERY AND JOY

"Do not be afraid."[1] This is the opening line from God's messenger each time the angel shows up in the Christmas story. To Zechariah, to Mary, to Joseph, to shepherds on a nighttime hill: "Do not be afraid" (Luke 1:13, 30; Matt 1:20; Luke 2:10). That is, of course, understandable. Most of us are not used to being interrupted by angels . . . at least, not in ways as clear and dramatic as was the case for those biblical characters.

Once assured they had nothing to worry about, each of those characters quickly moved from fear to mystery. "How shall I know this?" a confused Zechariah answered (Luke 1:18). "How shall this be, since I have no husband?" asked the teenaged Mary (Luke 1:34). The brokenhearted Joseph, who could not understand Mary's unexpected pregnancy, decided to "divorce her quietly" (Matt 1:19). "Let us go over to Bethlehem and see this thing that has happened," said the shepherds, who could not wrap their minds around the immensity of the "good news of a great joy" they had just heard (Luke 2:15, 10).

For those who played key roles in the first Christmas story, "mystery" was a key word. "Incarnation" was too big a concept to grasp. For most of us, it still is. But they could see and hold a baby,

---

1. To Joseph, the opening line is "Do not fear" (Matt 1:20). To the shepherds, the opening line is "Be not afraid" (Luke 2:10).

and that was enough to let them know that life would be different because that child had been born.

In a science class in undergraduate school, several of us liberal arts majors sat together in the back of the classroom. By "liberal arts" majors, I basically mean those of us who were math and science deficient. In my mind, the definition of a "logarithm" was "a tree being cut down to music." One day during a lecture about electricity (its sources, currents, manners of conduction, properties, power, uses, etc.), one of my math-and-science-challenged buddies asked the professor, "Dr. Johnson, can you explain all this to me exactly and simply? How does electricity work?" Our professor sighed and answered, "In your case, son, don't worry about how it works. Just be glad that it does."

How does electricity work? I don't know, but I celebrate the reality of light. How does love work? I don't know, but I celebrate the fact that it can capture us when we aren't looking for it (in romance or friendship, in holding babies or experiencing faith). How do you explain Christmas and the incarnation? I don't fully know. But I celebrate the fact that "to us a child is born" (Isa 9:6). A Messiah has come to walk where we walk and feel what we feel and, thus, to understand when we cry out to him from the darkness. That is the movement from mystery to joy.

My grandmother, a woman of deep personal faith, used to say about Christmas, "I don't understand why God chose an unmarried couple to have that baby. I don't understand why the wise men saw a star that nobody else seemed to notice. I don't understand why that innkeeper couldn't have made room for a pregnant woman. I don't understand why the angels told shepherds instead of rabbis. But this much I do understand: when God gave Jesus to the world, it was his way of saying, 'I love you.' That's all I need to know in order for every Christmas to be merry!" Mystery and joy. "The shepherds returned, glorifying and praising God for all the things they had heard and seen" (Luke 2:20), much of which was beyond their ability to interpret theologically.

A friend of mine has coached Little League baseball for years. Following a game a couple summers ago in which his team lost a heartbreaker in the final inning, his star pitcher sat on the bench in the dugout and cried. After all, he was not a major leaguer but rather a child struggling with disappointment. My friend, his coach, sat beside him. For a moment, he said nothing as the little boy tried to regain his composure. Then my friend spoke. "It hurts to lose a close one, doesn't it?"

The child sniffed and answered, "I can't understand it, Coach. We had it won. I don't know what happened." Mystery can be frightening and painful.

The coach continued. "We play again this week," he said. "Next week we play twice, once against the team that beat us today. I'm going to let you pitch that game. How many of those guys do you plan to strike out?"

The little boy began to smile. "I'll mow 'em down next week, Coach," he said. "They've not seen anything like I'm gonna throw at 'em!" Then the child stood to walk to the waiting van that would carry players to their homes. My friend said the child's smile grew even wider as he said, "You know, Coach, I love baseball!" The promise of a new chance at victory moved that child's mindset from mystery to joy.

"For to us [all of us] a child is born"! That was the promise made in Isaiah and repeated by angels to shepherds on a hillside overlooking Bethlehem (Isa 9:6; cf. Luke 2:11). Whether or not we understand the complex theological questions surrounding the incarnation, this much we do know: as my grandmother put it, when God gave Jesus to the world, it was God's way of saying "I love you." Maybe that is enough, even in the midst of mystery, to bring "good news of great joy"!

8

PRACTICAL INCARNATION

Saint Francis is one of the most beloved and venerated persons in Christian history. When the current pontiff was asked to take a papal name, he chose to become Pope Francis in honor of the diminutive man who lived in Assisi almost nine hundred years ago and taught that in giving to others, we become rich in spirit. Non-Roman Catholics, as well, honor his memory and teachings. In our backyard garden, my wife and I (lifelong Protestants) have not one but two statues of Francis, who was a patron saint of nature.

Saint Francis was a proponent of "incarnational theology." "Incarnation," of course, simply means "in the flesh." Francis believed that not only did God live in the flesh of Jesus, but he also lives in the flesh of everyone—each acquaintance, each neighbor, and each stranger along the way.[1]

Francis told a story many of us may find hard to wrap our minds around. But it was his story. So, allow me to simply share it as he told it without trying to dissect, construe, or demythologize. You can interpret it however you will. Francis was deathly afraid of leprosy, much as people in the eighties and nineties were afraid of AIDS or currently are afraid of COVID-19 or cancer. One day while riding, he rounded a bend near the woods and encountered

1. For more on Franciscan incarnational theology, see Nothwehr, "Franciscan View."

a leper. Predictably, Francis turned the horse to retreat in the other direction. But suddenly, he experienced the pain of guilt and believed that he heard a voice say to him, "Whatever you did to the least of these is what you did to me" (Matt 25:40). So, he returned to the leper, dismounted from his horse, bathed the man's wounds in a nearby river, hugged him (an expression of personal friendship), kissed his cheek (an expression of honor), and then got back on his horse to leave. When he turned to say goodbye, Francis claimed that the man had vanished.[2]

You and I may have trouble with that. We prefer to think that in all likelihood he went back to the river or walked off into the woods. Fine. But as already noted, this was Francis's experience. This is how he related the story. He believed the man had supernaturally disappeared. Francis was convinced that the leper on the road had been Jesus. In the saint's mind, Jesus had appeared to him to determine if Francis would run the risk of loving even if doing so was difficult or costly.

In the Christmas season, we make much of getting ourselves ready to receive the newborn King, of being sure that our mangers are clean and clear for his arrival. In truth, however, often even while we preach or teach or sing or pray about that topic, we fail to note that he arrives daily in a neighbor, a child, an acquaintance, or a person in need. The practical side of incarnation is not merely that God came in the flesh of Christ once upon a time but that Christ comes in the flesh of others *all* the time.

Practical incarnation, thus understood, clarifies that when we help others, we are expressing not just our love for them but also for the Christ who lives in them. Mother Teresa said that each dying beggar on the streets of Calcutta, cradled in her arms, was to her the dying body of her Lord.[3] In Jesus' parable of the judgment, the lambs (the faithful) ask, "Lord, when did we see thee hungry

2. See "Francis of Assisi." There are various versions of the story.

3. "Mother Teresa once led Bishop William Curlin of Charlotte, North Carolina, onto the streets of Calcutta after asking him if he wanted to meet Jesus. When they came upon a dying man, Mother Teresa knelt on the ground and embraced him in her arms and said, 'This is Jesus'" (Schaefer, "Mother Teresa," para. 5).

and feed thee, or thirsty and give thee drink? And when did we see thee a stranger and welcome thee, or naked and clothe thee?" (Matt 25:37–38). And the goats (the unfaithful) ask, "Lord, when did we see thee hungry or thirsty or a stranger or naked or sick or in prison, and did not minister to thee?" (Matt 25:44). And the Lord answers, "Truly, I say to you, as you did it [or did it not] to one of the least of these my brethren, you did it [or did it not] to me" (Matt 25:40; cf. 25:45).

That is practical incarnation. Whatever you do to support one institutionalized child who has no parents or whose home is unsafe or who suffers from serious developmental disabilities . . . Whatever you do to provide a protected haven for one spouse who has been abused by the other . . . Whatever you do to rescue one woman who has been the victim of trafficking . . . Whatever you do to make a dent in one organization's systemic racism . . . Whatever you do to shatter the darkness of one individual's loneliness with the light of your presence and love . . . Whatever you do to demonstrate kindness and civility to one person in an angry, divisive culture (especially to some person you might be tempted to ignore or push away) . . . Whatever you do to make one aged adult feel that the world has not forgotten them . . . Whatever you do via a phone call, email, or text to make one other person feel noticed and affirmed . . . is what you do to Christ himself. Incarnational theology says that every act of kindness to every other person is an expression of love to Jesus.

The flip side of the coin is that not only when we help others but also when they help us, we once again experience the Christ who lives in them.

Reflecting on how she survived the tragic and unexpected death of her husband, a woman told me of another lady who lived nearby. They were acquaintances at best, never having socialized together. However, one morning shortly after her loss, her doorbell rang. It was that neighbor, the mere acquaintance, carrying the predictable magi's gift of a casserole. She said when placing it on the table, "I know what you're going through. I lost my husband a few years ago. Maybe not having to cook dinner tonight will free you up to spend a little time with your kids . . . or with yourself."

After that, the same woman would show up once or twice a week at my friend's door. Sometimes, she would offer to take the children out, giving the grieving widow some much-needed alone time. On other occasions, she would come in bringing a container of imported coffee, pour two cups, and just sit and chat. "As often as not," my friend said, "'chat' actually meant that she would sit patiently and listen." While she never pushed religion on the woman who was walking "through the valley of the shadow of death" (Ps 23:4), she would often use the phrase "I'm praying for you." The new widow told me that she found inexpressible comfort from her neighbor. "In time," she said, "I came to look forward to those visits more than to anything else at all. Those were the moments when I didn't have to be strong for anyone—not for my children, not for my husband's grieving parents, not for anyone. I could fall apart safely, knowing she didn't judge me for it." She continued: "Later on, she helped me sort through memories, good ones and not-so-good ones, in my effort to process what had happened. She helped me learn to laugh about things. She restored a sense of hope for me, always saying, 'It will get better. I promise. I've been there.' I didn't know it then, but looking back, I know it now. Every time she came to my door, Jesus came with her."

In the practical nature of our day-to-day lives, how we treat others is how we treat Christ. And when others come to us with love and kindness, Christ himself comes with them.

9

KIDS IN THE SAME FAMILY

During his tenure in office, President Reagan once made the observation that perhaps it would take an attack from Mars for us at last to recognize that we are all members of the same family and this planet is the house where that one family lives. As it turns out, some forty years later, it wasn't Martians that made us consider our common humanity. It was, however, something almost as scary.

The COVID-19 pandemic reminded us that it is an equal-opportunity infector. It strikes anybody, not discriminating against Republicans or Democrats; men or women; Black, Brown, or White; northerners or southerners; Yankees or Red Sox; scientists or conspiracy theorists. It is equally interested in one and all. COVID-19 was a reminder of something we should have already known: that we really are all members of the same family, and this planet is the house where that one family lives.

Throughout the pandemic, a constant refrain has been "We're in this together!" That is a lesson that hopefully will not be forgotten post-pandemic. We are unwisely prone to separate from one another, to pigeonhole and categorize, allowing prejudice, bias, or ignorance about others to blur a vision of our shared humanness. The fact is, of course, that the phrase we hear so often is true: we really are "more alike than different." We are members of the same household, all in this thing and every other thing together. Thus,

God is calling us to reconcile, to embrace, to listen to one another, to learn, to love, and therefore, to survive.

Just from the standpoint of logic, if Jesus died for all, then he must also have been born for all. He was born for simple shepherds on a hillside and for three very wealthy magi from Persia. He was born for the venerated Mary and for the almost-anonymous Joseph. He was born for the prophets who predicted his arrival and for the innkeeper who locked the door to keep that arrival out. He was born for the Jews who for centuries had prayed for him to come and for the Roman soldiers in Bethlehem whose boots were planted firmly on the necks of those who had done the praying. He was born for Mary's cousin Elizabeth, whose unborn child danced within her when the prenatal Jesus entered her dwelling, and for Herod, who sought to murder Jesus once he had been delivered. Not all received him, welcomed him, understood him, or loved him. But all equally needed him and were at least provided the same opportunity to receive the sacred gift of Christmas that alone could meet their needs.

Put simply, we are all kids in the same family and thus share the common need for a Parent who will love and protect us.

Matthew devoted the ninth chapter of his Gospel to a journey Jesus made through a small area that had great needs. In that chapter of just thirty-eight verses, Matthew writes of Jesus healing a paralyzed man; showering compassion on "tax collectors and sinners," saying that he saw them as those who were sick and in need of a physician; raising from death the daughter of a leader of the synagogue; healing a woman who for twelve long years had suffered from a bleeding disorder that made her untouchable and thus separated her from those whom she loved; restoring sight to two men who were blind; and restoring the gift of speech to another man who was unable to talk. And that was just the beginning. Matthew continues: "Jesus went about all the cities and villages [of that region], teaching in their synagogues and preaching the gospel of the kingdom, and healing every disease and every infirmity" (Matt 9:35). Having addressed what Jesus did, Matthew then added one more brief and beautiful sentence explaining why he did it: "When he saw the crowds, he had compassion for them, because they were harassed and helpless, like sheep without a shepherd." (Matt 9:36). When Jesus looked at those people, he didn't see Pharisees, Sadducees, Essenes, Zealots, or people of the land.[1] He didn't visualize them divided into those five separate and historic Hebrew groups. He just saw them as kids in the same family, with needs they were unable to meet on their own and pains, hungers, fears, and tears. They needed a Parent who would love them, wash and bandage their wounds, comfort their crying, tenderly cradle them and sing lullabies, pass them a plate of food if they were hungry, and tuck them in with a reassuring story. "When he saw the crowds, he had compassion for them . . ." (Matt 9:36).

A friend who pastors a church with a large membership in Atlanta, Georgia, said to me, "During the lockdown, I began receiving emails from people who claimed they had forgotten how important church is until suddenly it was off-limits and they couldn't find another institution strong enough to comfort them. Even more importantly, they reported that they had come to realize in a new way how crucial God is when they couldn't find another power strong enough to protect them."

There is something critical during a pandemic or any other time about remembering that we are all just children in one big family and really do need and count on a Parent who loves us as such, who doesn't see and separate us as young or old; rich or poor; Black, Brown, or White; liberal or conservative; red or blue; or more than, less than, worse than, or better than. That loving Parent simply sees us as kids in the same household who are scared and vulnerable and need a protector who is "moved with compassion upon us."

Mary and Joseph, look up! Elizabeth and Zechariah, look up! Shepherds and wise men, innkeepers and Herod, rabbis and Roman soldiers, look up! One and all, look up to see the light of the star shining overhead. And listen for the song of angels. The

---

1. "People of the land" were one of the five groups of Hebrew people in the day and time of Jesus—it refers to the "common people" who were the majority in Israel but also had very little power (except in number).

one for whom you have longed and waited is coming "with healing in his wings" (Mal 4:2) for all his children. He sees us in our commonality and asks that we remove the artificial barriers we construct to shut out those who think, look, sound, vote, or act differently. He views us as kids in the same family, all equally loved by the same Parent whose nature is agape and who therefore calls us to love one another whether or not it's an easy thing to do. Look up, all you similar children with similar needs! The one you need most of all is coming at Christmas.

10

A LOVELY BIRTH
IN AN UNLOVELY WORLD

The Gospel of Matthew sets the Christmas story in the midst of personal confusion and political persecution. Put another way, it's not exactly a Rockettes performance or a Hallmark holiday movie. Matthew's world is the real, raw world in which we live.

The *confusion* part has to do with Joseph, Jesus' earthly father. When the angel shares his news, Joseph is understandably troubled by what he hears. Mary, his "betrothed" (which was a kind of legally binding engagement), is pregnant, and Joseph knows he's not the father. The woman he loves, with whom he has planned a future, whom he counts on and trusts, and who he believed loves him, too, apparently has been unfaithful. What else can he think? Obviously, he miscalculated her feelings for him. Perhaps it was an arranged marriage. Even so, it was one Joseph convinced himself was built on deep feelings that he and Mary had for one another. But now reality has come and the sad and shocking news that he has been mistaken. Mary is going to marry him, but clearly, she is in love with someone else.

Matthew says that "Joseph, being a just man and unwilling to put her to shame, resolved to divorce her quietly" (Matt 1:19) As already noted, betrothal did not simply mean that a couple planned to be married someday. Instead, it meant they had a legally binding understanding that such would be the case. Thus, to end a betrothal required a certificate of divorce from a Jewish priest. Joseph could have made it ugly. He could have spread the word throughout the tiny village of Nazareth that Mary lacked morals, that she had lied to him, that she was unfaithful. He could have ruined her reputation. In fact, according to the law of Moses, he could have had her stoned to death. But "Joseph, being a decent man, decided to divorce her quietly." He was confused. He felt he had been treated unfairly. But he still did not let his pain cause him to create pain for somebody else. "Joseph, being a decent man . . ."

The angel, of course, explained to Joseph that his fears were unfounded. "[The child] conceived in her is of the Holy Spirit," said the angel (Matt 1:20). And Joseph, no doubt still confused by the overwhelming nature of all that, took Mary as his own and the baby as his son.

There is more to the story as Matthew tells it than just confusion. Soon there would also be *persecution*. Within two years of the birth, wise men from the east knocked on Herod's door, asking, "Where is he who has been born king of the Jews? For we have seen his star in the East, and have come to worship him" (Matt 2:2). Herod was no more excited at the prospect of sharing his throne with someone else than Joseph had been at the prospect of sharing his bride's affection with someone else. So, Herod decided to have Jesus killed. Enter the same angel a second time—and by now, Joseph had learned to trust the angel's message whether or not he fully understood it. The message this time was to take Mary and the child and flee to Egypt under the cover of darkness in order to save the baby's life. Jesus began his earthly journey as an immigrant, an outsider. That may explain why toward the end, in the parable of the judgment, he chastises "the goats" (the unfaithful) by saying, "I was a stranger and you did not welcome me . . ." (Matt 25:43).

That is how the birth story is told by Matthew. The loveliest gift in all eternity was sent to a decidedly unlovely world, set in environments of confusion on one hand and persecution on the other. In other words, God's gift was given to a world not unlike our own. When Matthew wrote his Gospel, the Romans had done to Jerusalem what, in 2022, we witnessed Russia do to Ukraine. Leprosy was the great fear of the masses, even as COVID-19 has been recently and as cancer remains. We know about persecution and suffering. We see it daily.

The Christmas story speaks to us about the arrival of the "Prince of Peace" (Isa 9:6) and how he is born into lives that are not always peaceful but instead are wounded, weary, and worried. Matthew understood that, and so do we—that Christ is born into a world of struggles, suffering, sadness, and sorrows. But into that world he brings the gift of a new perspective. He does not take away all the pains and problems that are less than lovely, but he gives us eyes to see beauty in unlikely places.

A classmate of mine in college was a student I will refer to as Sam. Sam had been a victim of polio and walked only by virtue of having large, bulky metal braces on each leg and equally bulky metal crutches attached to each arm. He couldn't run or jog or walk briskly anywhere, ever. Instead, walking was slow and laborious for him, no doubt exhausting from having to lift heavy weights with every step. When the rest of us would go to dances, go hiking, or play sports, Sam stayed back at the dorm. The world was smaller and more confined for him. Frequently, he would go to medical appointments to deal with any number of issues that the rest of us never had to worry about at all. Even so, Sam was a person with a quick wit, a ready smile, and a positive attitude that would've made Norman Vincent Peale proud. One night just before Thanksgiving break, a number of us were sitting around the dorm discussing our plans for the holiday. The conversation led to the question "What do we have to be thankful for?" That morphed into "What happened today that made you thankful?" One by one, we replied. Some of the responses were funny, some sarcastic, some thoughtful and serious. All the while, Sam sat quietly listening, but also reading an assignment from a textbook. When it was his turn to answer, he said, "This morning, I got up . . . ," and we waited for him to finish the sentence. "This morning you got up, and what? What happened? What created for you a sense of thankfulness?" Instead, Sam surprised us. He said, "This morning, I got up," and then turned back to his textbook. In a shadowy world, one with pain and limitations, he had developed a perspective of light. He was thankful simply to be alive. "This morning, I got up!" By that we took him to mean: "I'm still here. I get another chance at this thing called 'life.' All may not be ideal for me; it may not be perfect—but this morning I got up! And I am thankful for that."

Joseph's world didn't change because of the birth. But every time Joseph looked at the baby, he knew that he had been changed. Blessed. An unlovely environment could not hide the loveliness of the child or the love Joseph felt for him.

That's what the holy birth does for us when we see it through Joseph's eyes. Christ's coming gives us strength to survive our challenges and perspective to understand that even amid them, there's still a lot to be thankful for.

11

SURPRISES

A husband decided one day on his way home from work to buy his wife a bouquet of roses. It was something he did for birthdays or anniversaries. On this particular day, however, he decided that an unexpected gift of beauty for no particular reason would be a symbol of his deep love for her. He walked through the front door of his house, bouquet in hand, where his wife spotted him from the den. "This has been the worst day ever!" she began before the door was fully closed behind him. "The kids have been totally out of control, fighting and breaking things. The dishwasher flooded the kitchen. The neighbor's dog dug up my tomato plants. And now you show up with flowers, so obviously you've done something you need to apologize for!"

Sometimes it's hard to properly interpret the moment when love takes us by surprise. Such was doubtless the case for Joseph.

"Now the birth of Jesus took place in this way," writes Matthew. "When his mother Mary had been betrothed to Joseph, before they came together she was found to be with child of the Holy Spirit" (Matt 1:18). That, to Joseph, was *a plan-changing surprise*. He assumed the young woman to whom he was engaged was someone who could be trusted, someone who loved him and only him. But now this . . . this unexpected and unwelcome news.

An acquaintance told me of his fifteenth anniversary at a growing company. He had a good track record and was head of the class in sales. The other employees liked and respected him. He knew that the director-of-marketing job was open and felt he had the inside track for it. The CEO gathered all the ranking staff together at 4:00 p.m. for a "special announcement."

My friend said, "We knew she would reveal the name of the new Director of Marketing. Some of my friends told me I was the obvious choice. I had earned it. No one else could match my record in the company. Though trying to be modest and deflect their praise, down deep I agreed with them. It had to be me. Furthermore, why else would the announcement be scheduled on that particular day, my fifteenth anniversary on the job?"

The CEO stood up and called the meeting to order. The room hushed. Sure enough, as all suspected, she said it was her privilege to announce who had been given the coveted position. My friend said, "I heard a name. It was surreal. I knew it had to be my name she called, but it wasn't. It was the name of a man who had been employed there half as long as I had. I was the one who had hired him, trained him, and supervised him. Now she had chosen him . . . over me." He reported going home that night angry, hurt, confused, and embarrassed. He fussed. He fumed. He wept. He said, "It was as if all the professional dreams I cherished most had been snatched away in one single moment." He experienced a plan-changing surprise.

"Being a just man and unwilling to put her to shame," Matthew's story says, Joseph "resolved to divorce her quietly" (Matt 1:19). In other words, no matter what he feared she had done to him, he would not do anything to embarrass her. "But," writes Matthew, "as he considered this, behold, an angel of the Lord appeared to him in a dream, saying, 'Joseph, son of David, do not fear to take Mary your wife, for that which is conceived in her is of the Holy Spirit'" (Matt 1:20). On the heels of a plan-changing surprise came *a mind-changing surprise*. Things were not as he had thought they were. He had not been betrayed. His love had not been rejected after all.

The epilogue to my friend's account of his disappointing fifteenth anniversary on the job is not unlike Joseph's story. After venting all his pain and hurt to his wife, he (like Joseph) "being a just man," decided to take the high road. He would resign, but he would do so with dignity. He would first go to the man who had been awarded the position he had desired for himself with congratulations. He would not complain to the CEO. He would quietly begin the search for a new job, and when he found one, he would resign. So, he returned to the office the next morning with his game face on. As decided, he went to the new Director of Marketing and congratulated him with a smile. He did his work as normally and effectively as he could, though his heart was not in it. As he prepared to go home late that afternoon, the CEO stepped into his office and closed the door. She laid a file folder on his desk and simply said, "Here's a job I need you to do. I want you to get on it as soon as possible." She never even asked if he was disappointed. She offered no explanation as to why he had been overlooked or passed by. She didn't speak a single word of gratitude about his fifteenth anniversary with the firm. It was simply "Here's a job I need you to do." He told me, "I couldn't even look her in the face, I was so hurt and confused." So, he picked up the folder and opened it. There was a page inside with a heading that read, "Job Description: Senior Vice President."

When he looked up at her, she was smiling. "You probably wanted the job I gave to someone else yesterday," she said. "But I believe you deserve something more than that."

He concluded his story by saying, "It was the only time in my life I've ever hugged my boss."

I don't know if Joseph hugged the angel—or if angels can be hugged. But I'll bet he wanted to. Just when the dream he cherished had been taken away, along came the mind-changing surprise that he would receive something even better.

"[Mary] will bear a son, and you shall call his name Jesus," said the angel, "for he will save his people from their sins" (Matt 1:21). With those words, Joseph experienced *a world-changing surprise.*

Our world needs that as much as Joseph's did. Our brokenness is undeniable. There is distrust and dissatisfaction, fear and
fatigue, anger and angst, heartache and hurt, want and weariness.
The world we know is very different from the one its Creator intended. All the way back to the Genesis story of Adam and Eve
succumbing to the temptation to know as much as God did,
Scripture contends that our brokenness results from our self-cen-
teredness. The word for that is "hubris," the desire to put self at the
very pinnacle of things. If my needs consistently take precedence
over everyone else's needs, and if enough people operate from that
mindset, then Eden is lost. Instead, we find a painfully inadequate
and often frightening world in its place.

But then comes Christmas and its world-changing surprise—
the surprise that there is an alternative way of doing business. British Prime Minister William Ewart Gladstone rightly said, "We look
forward to the time when the power of love will replace the love
of power. Then our world will know the blessings of peace."[1] In
this season, we welcome one whom Isaiah called "Prince of Peace"
(Isa 9:6). He tells us that there is a better way than our search for
power, possessions, and personal gain, a way which has the power
of love as its foundation. If heard and embraced by an audience
large enough, that becomes a world-changing surprise.

Matthew quotes Isaiah: "'Behold, a virgin shall conceive
and bear a son, and his name shall be called Emman'u-el' (which
means, God with us)" (Matt 1:23). In the end, it was *a life-changing
surprise*. "'His name shall be called Emman'u-el' (which means,
God with us'" (Matt 1:23).

In all the twists and turns of the mortal journey, on every
dark road, in every threatening midnight experience, when the
winds blow hard with ghostly voices, we do not make the journey
alone. "And the Word became flesh and dwelt among us," says John
(John 1:14). "Lo, I am with you always . . . ," said Jesus (Matt 28:20).
A church member who survived the bitter loss of a marriage, a
failed business, betrayal by one of her own children, and a physical illness that left her with impaired vision and reduced mobility,

1. William Ewart Gladstone, qtd. in Reed, "Love of Power," 14.

said to me, "I could not have made it through alone. That would have been categorically impossible. But every day I literally feel Jesus propping me up and holding me close. That's where I find the strength to keep putting one foot in front of the other. In fact, as odd as it may sound, there is a joy inside me now that I never had before." Emmanuel. God with us. Such is the source of a life-changing surprise.

Fear not, Joseph. However shadowy things may appear at the moment, bright and beautiful surprises are on the way.

12

TEMPORARY TERROR AND A LASTING MESSIAH

Following the indefensible attack on eighty public-health employees attending a Christmas party in San Bernadino a few years ago, a news reporter remarked that it was "a sad reminder that terrorism has finally reached our land." It is sad that terrorism is part of our country's landscape, and yet one has to wonder if that reporter had failed to pay proper attention. Had he not noticed Columbine, Virginia Tech, or Newtown; attacks at mosques or synagogues; 9/11, Pearl Harbor, the Jim Crow activities of the KKK, or slavery? A person I know described a famous serial killer as a man who made "unfortunate decisions with his life." I appreciated my friend's effort to show compassion, but my immediate thought was that wearing brown shoes with a black tuxedo is an "unfortunate decision." Murdering random strangers who have done you no harm and terrorizing an entire city for years is something far darker and more sinister than that. Terror is a sad reality in our land and in our world, and has been for a long, long time.

When John the Baptist preached a message about preparing the way for the Messiah's arrival, his listeners lived in what Isaiah had called "a land of deep darkness" (Isa 9:2). Herod, an emotionally unstable, ethically bankrupt, and politically powerful man, was on the throne of Israel. Concern for oneself that exceeds concern for one's citizens is toxic when applied to the outlook of a political leader. Furthermore, Israel was at that time occupied by the powerful and sometimes cruel Roman Empire. The people lived under a cloud of daily anxiety, and understandably so. They knew about terror.

John the Baptist borrowed some of Isaiah's language when he described the state of affairs in Israel while they waited for the Messiah to arrive—phrases like "wilderness," "valley," "rough places/ways," and "crooked" (John 1:23, Luke 3:5; cf. Isa 40:3–5, 59:8). Over against all that, however, he told his listeners not to surrender to terror, not to give up on a future that would be brighter than their present day. "Make straight the way of the Lord," he said to them, quoting Isaiah (John 1:23). Make way for someone who is bigger and stronger than Herod or Caesar, someone who can bring God's salvation to the people of the land. John was preaching two thousand years ago, but his words are just as timely now as they were then.

Two things can be noted in response to John's message. First, you and I cannot fix the world, *but we know someone who can.* We can be positive influences through things like votes and voices, prayers to God, and petitions to those who govern. But individually, we cannot fix the world. Like John, however, we believe someone is coming who does possess that power.

Herod and Caesar Augustus did not last. Hitler and Stalin did not last. Vladimir Putin will not last. Whatever politician you fear the most will not last. His time on the world's stage will end. But God and truth and freedom and love and the power of Jesus will live on. "Make straight the way of the Lord," proclaimed his first cousin John, declaring that when he arrived, all people would see God's salvation (deliverance) (John 1:3).

"Wishful thinking," we respond. "A pretty dream, but at the end of the day, it's just so much religious babbling," we fear. Those responses ignore the lessons of history. Rome occupied Israel, persecuted Christianity, and even executed Jesus. But less than three hundred years later, the empire adopted Christianity as its official religion. Still today, the majority of the world's Christians view

Rome as their spiritual capital city. Herod and Augustus did not last. The terror of their age eventually ended. "Prepare ye the way," said John. "Get ready. One is soon to come, and because of him all people will see God's salvation." Do not give up on this wounded world. And do not become resigned to it either. Stand up. Speak out. But also know that you and I cannot ultimately repair all that is broken. However, Advent says one is on the way who can.

Second, *I do have certain power*, and part of that is to make myself ready for the one who is to come, to personally "prepare the way" for his arrival.

Advent is about that. It is about refusing to jump from the Macy's Thanksgiving Day Parade directly to Christmas morning. Instead, Advent is a season for preparing, for pondering, for thinking seriously about who Christ is, what his arrival can mean for us, and what is required to make ourselves ready.

- As such, preparing the way involves *self-assessment*. "What stands between my life and my Lord, and what am I going to do about it?"

- It requires *repentance*. "I regret living in such fashion as to disappoint him, to either harm or ignore neighbors, and to cheat myself out of meaning and joy. What does changing directions (the biblical definition of the word 'conversion') demand of me?"

- It requires *attitudinal adjustments*. "What lesser things have I allowed to take center stage in my life, edging the most important thing(s) out?" When Scrooge tells Marley that he was good at business, Marley's response that people were supposed to have been his business was a response about the dire results of misshapen priorities.[1]

- It requires *openness*. Receiving Jesus can be an intimidating thing because we are never quite sure what he may ask of us if we do. "Behold, I stand at the door and knock" (Rev 3:20). Part of us wants to unlock the door. But another part fears

1. Dickens, *Christmas Carol*, 29.

that rather than entering to be with us, he will ask that we exit to follow him.

Preparing the way is not easy work. But without it, the holiday comes and goes devoid of the real, transforming, empowering arrival of the Messiah.

Ours is a frightening world. But its story is not yet concluded. Martin Luther King Jr. was correct when he stated that "the arc of the moral universe is long, but it bends toward justice."[2] We are on a journey. Whatever the present moment may contain and however daunting that may be, this is not the first time people have felt fear or despair. We do what we can to combat evil and advocate for good, all the while aware that we do not have the power to make all things different. Advent, however, says we don't give up, because we know someone is on the way who does have that power. Those with a sense of history can see how he has changed things vastly over two millennia. Thus, those with a sense of faith are confident that he will continue to do so during the long arc of time.

And so we wait—a fundamental part of what the word "Advent" means. We wait, but we do so creatively. Proactively. Personally. Spiritually. We do not just sit and wait. Rather, we do the work of the soul that is required to prepare the way for the one who is coming. And come he will to a world or any individual that is paying attention.

2. King, "Remaining Awake," para. 63.

13

GIFTS

Most of us have received countless gifts across Christmas seasons past. Some are remembered for their grandeur. Your first car shortly after receiving your driver's license. A diamond ring from the man you married and with whom you have built a life. Some are remembered for their sentiment. The scarf your grandmother knitted on what you did not know at the time would be her last Christmas. A crayon portrait of the manger scene that is still taped to your refrigerator, though the kindergarten-aged child who gave it to you is now grown with children of her own. Some are remembered because they were what we needed most, whether or not we realized it at the time. A puppy that became your closest friend and confidant as you navigated the difficult and often lonely waters of adolescence. A bus ticket to a campus where you would prepare for the professional life in which you now spend the majority of your waking hours.

I have, as have most, received gifts that were of little use. Sweaters that were too large or too small. Gift certificates to places that went out of business before I could redeem them. Books about subjects that were of no interest to me whatsoever. And, even as an enthusiastic foodie, boxes or plates with beautiful bows that contained (in my opinion) less than beautiful foods—things like fruitcake, jerky, or anything containing rhubarb.

A baby in Bethlehem long ago, probably only a toddler when the magi arrived at his parents' house, had little use for gold, frankincense, or myrrh. Gold, to be sure, is grand. Frankincense is sentimental for those who appreciate the symbolism of liturgy. And myrrh, in that context, was of little use at all to anyone who was alive. But each gift constituted a memory for him as he grew into adulthood: the gift of gold indicating respect offered to him as a king; the gift of frankincense, a reminder of the mystery of worship and of the nearness of the divine, mysterious one; the gift of myrrh symbolizing that which would come but would be passionately resisted with the prayer "Father, if it be possible, let this cup pass from me" (Matt 26:39).

Gifts received at Christmas point us toward other things. Most of all, they point us toward the givers and the love represented in what was given. Even the fruitcakes, jerky, and rhubarb pies came from hands of kindness and hearts of love, some of whom have been gone for years. But their memories remain, as does my gratitude for the gestures of friendship they so sweetly offered.

On my very first Sunday as a pastor following graduation from seminary, I stood nervously to proclaim "good news of great joy" (Luke 2:10). I was twenty-five years old, unmarried, and seriously inexperienced. I had learned a lot about the Bible but had not yet put in enough years to learn much about life. Before me sat a room full of strangers. Many had lived long and difficult years. They had been in places I had not been and witnessed things I had not seen. They had known both celebrations and suffering as yet unknown in my life. I had no idea what they expected from me, but I assumed it was probably more than I was equipped to offer. I recall the anxiety of that day, a deep-down sense of fear that I could not provide what was most needed by those folks whose names and stories I did not know. Later on, after living among them for years, I realized there had been no need for fear. They were as kind and nurturing as people can be. They gently took their novice pastor into their arms and loved and prayed for and surrounded me with indescribable and undeserved goodness. But on that first Sunday, I had no way of knowing what they were like. I only knew that I was surrounded by strangers and needed a visible source of strength greater than my own.

Gazing out from the pulpit, I spotted a familiar face seated on a pew to the right of the center aisle at the very rear of the sanctuary. Dr. John Carlton, my seminary professor of preaching, a brilliant, well-published scholar, had driven seventy miles from campus to a small brick church on a hillside in a southern mill town to support a former student. He knew how stressful that first Sunday can be. He understood how lonely a pastor can feel when there's not a face seated in the congregation to which he or she can attach a name. He knew I would stand behind the pulpit that day weak-kneed and sweating beneath a preacher's robe. And so, he came to offer silent support and provide a calming smile, one I could turn to as a fledgling preacher that stressful morning—one whose eyes would meet mine with encouragement and whose nod would affirm his confidence that I could do what I feared was beyond my reach. It was a gift of inestimable value, one that all these years later I still remember with deep thanks.

"Gratitude bestows reverence," wrote Sarah Ban Breathnach, "allowing us to encounter everyday epiphanies, those transcendent moments of awe that change forever how we experience life and the world."[1] Gratitude, of course, requires the spiritual sensitivity to recognize a gift when it comes. However it comes. Through whomever it comes. Even when we don't fully understand what it means when it comes. Gold. Frankincense. Myrrh. Hand-knitted scarves. Fruitcakes. An unexpected face in a room full of strangers. Incarnation. "To you is born this day in the city of David a Savior . . ." (Luke 2:11). Gifts, whether large or small, expensive or from a bargain basement, represent the love someone feels for your life. It is what the gift represents that we ultimately remember, and this, as Breathnach wrote, "change[s] forever how we experience life and the world."

There is this other thing. The rich meaning of Christmas is discovered not only in each gift that we receive but also in each moment when our life becomes a gift to someone else. Every time

---

1. Breathnach, *Simple Abundance*, 2.

we do or say or offer or become something that brings light to some other person's world, we understand at a deeper level that which is inherent in the words "good news of great joy." Certainly, that is at least part of the reason why there is a single verse that appears in the holy books of every one of the world's great faiths: "So whatever you wish that men would do to you, do so to them" (Matt 7:12). It is as if all people who seek for God, whatever path they follow, intuitively know that one same thing—that a blessed life is just as much dependent on what we give away as on what we receive. "The greatest Christmas gifts I obtain," said a woman to me, "are the smiles I see on the faces of the hungry folks at the local shelter when I place food on their empty plates. You couldn't buy me anything at Saks that could be as valuable as that."

Gifts, large or small, are symbols of love. When we are the givers, we experience the joy of knowing that we have made another life better or brighter. When we are the recipients, we experience the beauty of knowing that we are not alone or unnoticed as we make our way along the path. In terms of faith, that is both the end and the beginning of the Christmas story. The biblical story ends with the awareness that "God so loved the world that he gave his only Son" to us (John 3:16). That ignites the beginning of our own stories where we seek, in response, to express gratitude by giving grace and kindness to others in the name of one who came to Bethlehem and gave life in unimagined fullness to us.

PART 3

The Readers

I ALWAYS TELL MY seminary homiletics students that each time they preach, there is one thing they can count on. At some point during the sermon, those who are still awake and listening will ask, "So what?" For some, the question will be posed a minute or two into the sermon. For others, it may come at the very conclusion. But for all, somewhere along the way, that question will be asked. "So, what does anything you are talking about have to do with me? My life? My situation? My family (whatever form that takes)? My sense of personal meaning (or lack thereof)? My journey in my right-now world?" A sermon that merely imparts information, however important, is not a sermon at all. It is instead a lecture. Sermons are designed to bridge the gap between the world of the biblical writers and the world of the current-day listeners who sit in the pews.

The very same thing is true for those who read devotional literature. To be educated about Scripture and its prevailing themes is a good thing. However, biblical themes become transformational only when readers are able to answer the "So what?" question. That is the difference between a textbook and a devotional book.

There are Gospel writers. There is a central message. But for an Advent/Christmas devotional book to have a meaningful impact, the central message articulated by those Gospel authors has to resonate with readers in some personal and practical way. Let's take a look at a few of the ways that *the* story can become *our own*.

14

WAITING

Standing in the narthex one Sunday a few years ago, speaking with worshipers as they exited onto Fifth Avenue, I was greeted by a woman who shook my hand and said kindly, "That was a good sermon."

Trying to be gracious and appropriately humble, I answered, "Thank you, but God did it."

To which she replied, "It wasn't that good!"

I suppose we are all guilty of hoping for things that may be a bit beyond our reach.

Certainly, such seemed to be the case for the people of Israel eons ago. They hoped that God would send the Messiah. They prayed for it. They longed for it. They looked for it. They talked about it. And they waited . . . and waited . . . and waited until they wondered if his arrival was something beyond their reach.

We all know that in addition to Santa, we parents get to give a gift or two to our children. I remember the December I was in second grade. My hero then was Robin Hood. Obviously, things change, as my heroes now are Ina Garten and Guy Fieri. Back then, though, I idolized Robin, Little John, Friar Tuck, and all those sword-swinging, merry men in Sherwood Forest. For Christmas that year, all I wanted was a sword so that I could pretend to be one of them. One afternoon following school, my friend Tommy came over. It was raining that day, forcing us to amuse ourselves indoors. At one point, we were tossing a Wiffle ball back and forth in the hall. One of us failed to catch it, whereupon it rolled into my parents' room and beneath their bed. So, Tommy and I went in to retrieve it. Hidden away beneath their bed, we found a large box, unopened, with these words written on it: "Junior Fencing Set." Apparently, that was as close as they could get to a sword like Robin's. Inside the box was not one sword but two. Not one mask but two. It would have made the merry men green with envy. Tommy and I fenced our way through half the afternoon, Robin and Little John defeating the Sheriff of Nottingham. Then, however, we were forced to carefully replace the items in the box so that my parents would not know it had been discovered. Furthermore, for the next two weeks, I had to act as if I didn't know it was there. Those were the longest two weeks of my childhood, enduring the holiday but not celebrating it, impatiently waiting for Christmas morning, which inched its way toward me at a snail's pace.

Isaiah's audience would have resonated with my childhood emotions. Five to six hundred years before the Messiah finally arrived, Isaiah looked toward the skies and pleaded, "O that thou wouldst rend the heavens and come down . . . to make thy name known" (Isa 64:1–2). The people had spent almost a full century exiled in Babylon (modern-day Iraq). And even after the exile ended, they would still live in the shadows and with the threats of Egypt, Syria, Assyria, and Rome. For six hundred more years, they would keep praying that the skies would open and the Deliverer would come. "O, that you would rend the heavens and come down . . . to make yourself known among us."

So, what happens when we wait and long for something with all our hearts and souls? Apparently, Isaiah thought waiting is not so much an experience of endurance as it is an experience of preparation.

Last December on Christmas Eve, I witnessed one individual plus another couple shopping for trees at an almost-empty lot not far from where I live. I jokingly remarked to my wife, "What's their rush? They've got another ten or twelve hours before Christmas gets here!" Maybe they simply were observing the tradition as it began, with a tree being placed in the home and decorated on Christmas Eve and then the residents living in its light for the next twelve days. Let's give them the benefit of the doubt. It appeared, however, that they were people who had suddenly encountered the day but had missed the season that preceded it.

Advent is about waiting expectantly, prayerfully, creatively. It's about a journey toward an event without which the event itself cannot be fully understood or appreciated.

One of the Mannings (I can't remember if it was Peyton or Eli) made the statement that he loved each minute on the field as much as he hated each hour in the training room. But without the weight lifting and muscle stretching and body toning, he said, he would not have been able to succeed as a quarterback. Whichever brother made the statement, it came from someone who had won two Super Bowls and was observing that you don't just suit up and play the game. Instead, you prepare, you make yourself ready, you do the hard work of creative waiting. God "works for those [with those] who wait," wrote Isaiah (64:4)—those who seek to properly prepare themselves and make room for that which they desire most of all.

Do I want peace? Jesus said that requires some work on my part. "Blessed are the peacemakers," he said (Matt 5:9). A woman I know received an early-December phone call from her daughter in another state. "Mom," the daughter said, "I never know what to get you for Christmas. So this year, I just decided to phone and ask. What would you like as your gift?" The mother answered, "This year, I want peace. That's it. Just peace. So if you and your husband plan to fuss and fight throughout your entire visit this Christmas like you did last year, then I'd rather you spent the time visiting his parents instead." Funny? Yes. But honest? I suspect it was straight from the heart.

Do I want peace internally or in my external relationships? If so, then it is imperative that I step back from the stress and anger that invades our world too much of the time, that I create an oasis, that I focus on the calm and quiet "Silent Night" side of the manger story, that I meditate, pray, and refuse to allow the angst of others to interrupt my effort to make or discover peace.

Do I want friendship at Christmas? Then maybe that requires my seeking to be a better friend to others. Both the Bible and plain common sense remind me that "whatever a man sows, that he will also reap" (Gal 6:7).

Do I want kindness in my world (i.e., do I want people to treat me more kindly)? Then maybe I need sufficient self-discipline in what I do and say and post on social media to express kindness (not hostility) to others. Once again, "whatever a man sows, that he will also reap."

Do I want happiness? Then maybe I should intentionally look for the blessings and bright spots that still exist in my world but rarely make the evening news. It could be that I ought to take a second look at the ugly tie I have received but will never wear and the tasteless fruitcake I am given but will never eat and see them for what they are—reminders that someone cares enough about me to offer a gift.

Do I want a deeper sense of meaning? Then maybe I should change the way I pray in December, no longer making prayer a wish list for a cosmic Santa ("God, here's what I want from you") but rather an experience of silence where I simply say, "God, what do you want from me?" Then say nothing more, but faithfully wait for an answer to come.

God "works for those [with those] who wait for him," says Isaiah (Isa 64:4). Throughout December, people ask, "Are you ready for Christmas?" When we reply, "My goodness, no, I'm not even close," that is the right answer. Only in the long, slow, soulful process of spiritual waiting is it possible to be ready for Christmas when the day at last arrives.

15

WAITING FOR ONE
WHO COMES TO REIGN

Who do you answer to in life? Who holds you accountable?

A man complained to me about his supervisor at work, using these words: "I envy a person with a job like yours. When you're the senior minister of a church, you don't have to answer to anybody."

I replied, "You know I'm married, right?" He smiled, after which I continued by informing him that I had over five thousand church members in my congregation and far, far more than that who watched me via livestreaming and thought of me as their pastor. "I work for them all," I told him, "and they all have wants and needs and ideas about how my work should be done. Most of all, there's Jesus. When it's easy and when it's the total opposite of easy, I work for him. He is my supervisor."

None of us makes all our decisions without regard to somebody else. We all answer to someone. We are held accountable by employers, employees, and customers. We pay taxes to the government and obey the laws of the land. As people of faith, we primarily answer to God. God's will (supposedly, at least) shapes and fashions our actions. And for Christians, that will is most clearly understood through the life and teachings and challenges and commands of Jesus.

Isn't that ultimately what Christmas is about? To be sure, the warm and fuzzy part about a baby in a manger—"the little Lord Jesus asleep on the hay"—is important. But more important is the realization that the little Lord Jesus grew up. He grew up into someone who made (and still makes) all manners of difficult demands.

> And the angel said to her, "Do not be afraid, Mary, for you have found favor with God. And behold, you will conceive in your womb and bear a son, and you shall call his name Jesus.
> He will be great, and will be called the Son of the Most High;
> and the Lord God will give to him the throne of his father David,
> and he will reign over the house of Jacob for ever;
> and of his kingdom there will be no end." (Luke 1:30–33)

"He will reign . . . forever." The infant child, said the angel, will become the eternal King who will issue strong and often difficult commands. For example:

- "You, therefore, must be perfect, as your heavenly Father is perfect" (Matt 5:48).
- "Sell what you possess and give to the poor" (Matt 19:21).
- "If any man would come after me, let him deny himself and take up his cross and follow me" (Matt 16:24).
- "Judge not, that you be not judged" (Matt 7:1).
- "Go, and do not sin again" (John 8:11).

On and on they go—those strong and serious statements from the baby who grew up to become "King of kings" (1 Tim 6:15). "He will reign . . . for ever" (Luke 1:33), and in so doing will ask us to go places and do things we would not have chosen on our own.

For example, the grown-up Jesus commands that the plights and pains of children not be ignored: "Let the children come to me, and do not hinder them; for to such belongs the kingdom of God" (Luke 18:16).

It is too easy in our hectic world to forget the staggering number of children who go to school hungry every day, who sleep beneath bridges every night, or who suffer abuse at the hands of an adult authority figure. Those who have no vote in their well-being and no power to escape their pain are confined in dark, dim mangers. Someone is called to be their advocate, to speak for those who have no voice. The old adage confronts us all: "If not this, what? If not now, when? If not me, who?"

What list of biblical commands that are difficult could leave this off: "Love your enemies . . . For if you love those who love you, what reward have you?" Jesus said. "And if you salute only your brethren, what more are you doing than others? Do not even the Gentiles do the same?" (Matt 5:44, 46–47)?

A woman in Tucson left a holiday cake on the doorstep of a neighbor, an older, curmudgeonly man who was a thorn in her flesh. Her blood pressure spiked every time she merely saw him drive by in his car. But it was Christmas and, whether from faith or from guilt, she felt the need to do something "seasonally nice" (her words). So, she left the cake and a card simply saying, "Merry Christmas!" The next morning, her doorbell rang. On the front porch was the curmudgeon with her uncut cake in hand.

"You left this for me?" he said.

"Yes," she answered (already feeling the old anger begin to rise).

There followed a moment's silence, then he continued. "When my wife died, you didn't say anything. A few of the other neighbors on this street did, but you acted like nothing happened. I've been angry at you ever since."

More silence. "Then that's why twice in homeowners' association meetings you blocked our renovation plans," she countered. "I've been angry at you ever since." Again, silence. "So you're returning the cake. You're right, it was a bad idea," she told him.

But he replied, "I'm not giving it back. I'm *bringing* it back. I thought maybe it was time we should eat it together."

She invited him in, where they sat over cake and coffee and talked. At first they spoke of the anger each had felt toward the other. But then they spoke of other things: family, the neighborhood they shared, their lives and dreams and pains. She said, "That morning he came into my home an enemy, but he went back to his home a friend. Four years later, as he lay in a hospital bed dying, I was the person he sent for. Mine was the last face he saw before closing his eyes for the final time. When he changed worlds, he did so with his hand in mine. That memory has always been my Christmas miracle."

"For if you love those who love you, what reward have you?" said Jesus. "Do not even the Gentiles do the same?" (Matt 5:46–47).

"Do not be faithless, but believing" (John 20:27). There's another command that is not always easy to obey. It may not sound like too much of a challenge, but it is. Jesus spoke those words to Thomas, who had said to the other disciples, "Unless I see in his hands the print of the nails, and place my finger in the mark of the nails, and place my hand in his side, I will not believe" (John 20:25). Thomas feared that at the cross, the world had won, sin had prevailed, and evil had emerged victorious. We understand those emotions. It's impossible not to become a doubting Thomas from time to time. When simply looking around and seeing COVID-19, cancer, hatred, prejudice, fear, Putin's aggression in Ukraine, North Korea, Syria, Iran, or the great political chasm in our own land fueled by extremist philosophies both on the right and on the left, it is difficult not to wonder if the world, sin, and evil have not emerged triumphant. At a holiday party, the host asked all of us gathered there to answer one question: "What do you want in the new year?" One at a time we answered, some sentimentally and others humorously. However, when it came to his turn, an aging minister in attendance replied neither sentimentally nor with humor. He said, "I want some stretches of time in the coming months when the morning news does not assault us." Most of us are quick to add our own "amen" to his words. So, along comes grown-up Jesus and says, "Be of good cheer, I have overcome the world" (John 16:33). Jesus is bigger and stronger than it is. For two thousand years, the faces and forces of evil have come and now are all gone. But he and the movement he started remain. If he reigns over us, then he asks something incredibly difficult of us. He asks us to trust, to believe even in the shadowy times that no matter how big or frightening the world may seem, he is bigger and he will prevail.

Making it personal, which at some level faith always is, means understanding that not only is the Messiah bigger than the world out there but he is also big enough and strong enough to help us cope with and overcome whatever the world throws our way. Whatever hurts or heartaches or guilt or grief or disappointments or despair one is coping with, it is no match for him.

In the first church I served after graduating from seminary, I came to know a man named Frank. He never missed a Sunday at worship. He was always exceedingly kind to me, supportive of and encouraging to a young and inexperienced preacher taking his first toddling steps. Frank worked in a cotton mill five days a week, his lungs increasingly affected by the fiber mist he breathed eight hours a day. He was not able, financially or physically, to afford or enjoy things so many simply take for granted. He couldn't afford to join a fitness center or play golf or have a weekend house at the lake. His form of relaxation was to sit in a folding chair at the edge of his lawn at the end of workdays, to watch the traffic rushing by on the highway a block from his house, and to fantasize about the places they might be going which he would never see. And yet, Frank seemed at peace with life, satisfied and happy. One day, he made a passing comment that helped me understand how he maintained so positive an outlook in his not-always-positive world. He said, "I'm a Christmas kind of guy. I've spent my whole life in a variety of mangers. But I have always known who shares those mangers with me." Sometimes it is easier to sink with Thomas than to stand with Frank. But the baby who grew up asks us to trust that he will enter the manger moments of our lives and give us strength to survive.

The baby grew up. That is the challenging part of the story. However, it is the comforting part as well.

16

WAITING FOR PEACE

A story made the rounds a few years ago about a man who inherited a ski chalet outside Jackson Hole, Wyoming, from a long-lost uncle. Those things usually occur only in movies, but for the man and his family, it occurred in real life. He and his wife were grateful and excited when they first received the news . . . until they made their initial visit to see their new property. There they discovered an old house (not deserving the name "chalet" in any fashion imaginable). It had drafty windows, a leaking roof, and old wiring and plumbing, all of which had to be replaced, and a narrow, steep, and winding driveway that made the house almost inaccessible in winter weather. The nephew said, "I thought we were getting a palace. Instead, we were given a money pit. We could have built a chalet for less than it cost to repair that old house which was about to fall in."

We all know that feeling. We have all waited, hoped, and prayed for a promotion at work. Or a new job. Or the right car. Or a better apartment. Or a more exciting romantic partner. Or for that special Amazon package to arrive with the dress that looked so good in the catalog or the new tool that promised to do so many tasks in half the time with half the effort. We've all taken the first bite of a dessert placed before us, mouths watering to taste that luscious strawberry pie, only to discover it was rhubarb. We know what it's like for our expectations to exceed the nature of the reality that finally comes.

The Hebrew people understood how it felt to wait and hope and pray during four generations of Babylonian captivity. They waited to be liberated. They prayed to be returned home to Jerusalem. Finally, due to King Cyrus of Persia, the long-desired day came. Babylon the Great had fallen. The people of Israel returned home. It was a time of irrepressible optimism and joy. So said the psalmist: "When the LORD restored the fortunes of Zion, we were like those who dreamed. Then our mouth was filled with laughter, and our tongue with shouts of joy" (Ps 126:1–2).

"Like those who dreamed . . ." For them, it was literally a dream come true. What on earth could be better? But sometimes when we receive what we dreamed for, prayed for, and waited for, it's not all we hoped it would be.

Upon their return home, the people found that Jerusalem had become a city without effective leadership. Everything had fallen into serious disrepair. The temple had been destroyed. Jerusalem was effectively bankrupt in terms of money, industry, and resources. Suddenly those returning realized that, in fact, they had gone from tough times to a whole new set of times almost as tough. So, the psalmist prayed a new prayer. He articulated a new dream. It was the prayer and dream for the arrival of a Messiah who could restore that which had all but caved in. "Restore our fortunes, O LORD," he wrote, "[so that] those who sow in tears reap with shouts of joy!" (Ps 126:4–5).[1]

For two millennia, we have celebrated the angels' song of "Glory to God in the highest, and on earth peace among men with whom he is pleased!" (Luke 2:14). But when we take a look around, our new Jerusalem is not what we'd hoped it would be. Instead of peace and goodwill, we find fears and frustrations, divisions and despair, invasions and injustice, acrimony and anger. Though sufficient food is produced to feed everyone on earth bountifully, over eight hundred million are food and nutrition deprived to the

---

1. The account of the return of the Hebrews from Babylonian captivity is described in Jer 20–22, 24–29, 32.

point that their physical well-being is endangered. Anti-Semitism is rearing its head in new and disturbing ways, even in European countries that should remember the horrors of the Holocaust. Putin savaged the nation of Ukraine, and now all Eastern Europe sleeps with one eye open wondering who might be next. Here at home we witness racism, gender inequity, the abuse or neglect of both children and the aged, trafficking, gun violence, the decline of institutional religion, increasing suicide rates among the young, partisanship that erodes patriotism, an us-against-them mindset that does the work of our global enemies for them, and fears about what new pandemic may be waiting around the next corner. This place we inhabit is not Eden. Our home, like Jerusalem in the days when the people returned from Babylon, is not what we had hoped for.

So, what do we do? We do what they did 2,500 years ago. We cry out to the heavens, "Restore our fortunes, O LORD . . . [so that] those who sow in tears reap with shouts of joy!" (Ps 126:4–5). In this fractured, frightened world, O Lord, send a Messiah who can bring us peace. Send us a new Christmas and a new choir of angels that can make our dream come true, the dream of "peace [on earth] among men with whom he is pleased!" (Luke 2:14).

What if the angels answer, "You have a role in it, too, you know. You will receive peace when you make peace"? The returnees to Jerusalem were not able to merely pray and wait. Their actions were part of the answer to their prayers. The fortunes of Jerusalem were restored only when, in partnership with God, they rolled up their sleeves and went to work.

Do I worry about anger and divisiveness? Then I shouldn't fan those flames with my own social media posts. Did my heart break when I saw the film footage coming from Ukraine with moms and children uprooted from their homes, seeking safety and shelter in Poland? Then I have the opportunity to make contributions to humanitarian agencies seeking to assist the refugees. Do I lament the issues that keep sane people awake at night? Then I need to search for a more restful life by taking more concrete actions regarding those issues: by sending a letter to my congressman, by volunteering some time to a local helping agency, by making a contribution, by recycling, by tutoring a child, by advocating for the elderly or disabled, by joining a prayer vigil. I am simply called to do what I can where I can when I can, and a renewed sense of personal peace will be the outcome. A woman said to me, "I cannot change the world. But I have found that I can be there for one person at a time—one person who is sick, grieving, lonely, or frightened. I cannot change the world, but I can change that person's world. And by doing so across a long number of years, my own world has been changed."

In addition to our activity, there is the greater reality of God's activity. To find peace requires an openness to the Prince of Peace.

The angels said to impoverished shepherds in a nation occupied by hostile oppressors on a night when it seemed there was no peace to be found, "Behold, I bring you good news of a great joy" (Luke 2:10). In their immediate context, those words didn't seem to make sense. But the angels knew what those shepherds had yet to learn, that one had been born who brought with him power and potential and promise greater than the world's ability to derail it. Such is still the truth about the one who came at Christmas long ago and still comes to us in this present age. To give up on that, even when times are less than ideal, is to allow the world to win. If the evil of any given moment numbs us to the beauty of the Bethlehem moment, then Herod is victorious.

Howard Thurman, the brilliant late professor at Boston University who was an esteemed theologian, a great preacher, and the mentor of Martin Luther King Jr. in the pre-civil rights era, says in a poem that the nativity is not the stopping place. It is instead a starting place, pointing toward the work of healing that will one day bring victory.[2] Confidence in that not-yet-but-on-the-way victory enables us to sing for joy even in the midst of tears.

Do what you can to make peace, and you will find peace. Claim the angel's promise that a Prince of Peace is born almost always in the midst of tears. Our world, like Jerusalem when the Hebrews returned from Babylon, is not perfect yet. Life's temple

2. See Thurman, "Work of Christmas."

has not been completed. The pains and problems are not resolved. But we believe that one is coming who can lead us from where we are to where we need to be, and so we wait and pray with those who also waited and prayed long ago. "Restore our fortunes, O Lord . . . [so that] those who sow in tears reap with shouts of joy!" (Ps 126:4–5).

17

ADVENT, BUSYNESS, AND SEEING THE MAIN THING

It was mid-December. Our clergy staff walked into a lovely restaurant on Madison Avenue for our weekly lunch meeting. The restaurant was about a block from our church and regularly attracted large numbers of tourists. Upon entering, we spotted what we often saw in late December or early June—a group of students seated together at a table near the front of the dining area. During those two seasons of the year, you would see lots of similar groups—young people who had probably been sent to New York City as a Christmas present or graduation gift from Mom and Dad. Four of them were sitting together that cold, clear day in Advent. There they were, gathered at a table in of one of New York's finest culinary establishments, surrounded by the bustle and energy of midtown Manhattan, never knowing if they were about to see a movie star or rock entertainer or world leader walk in and sit at the table next to them or pass by outside the window. Yet, all four young people who were sitting there with the world at their fingertips were staring down while busily typing on their cell phones. They were unaware of the city, unaware of the people around them, unaware of the friends who were sharing that same moment which had never been before and would never come again, unaware that the parents who had scraped together enough money to make their trip possible might just as well have sent the four of them to a nearby McDonald's in any little local hamlet from Maine to New Mexico. You can access Instagram or TikTok on your phones just as easily and a lot more cheaply there.

Stephen Covey, author of *The 7 Habits of Highly Effective People*, says, "The main thing is to keep the main thing the main thing."[1] The wise men understood the need from time to time to let everything else go in order to focus on one main thing. "Where is he who has been born king of the Jews? For we have . . . come to worship him" (Matt 2:2). The shepherds did the same. With the sheep safely locked in their corral, they departed from their hillside, leaving momentary tasks behind and saying, "Let us go over to Bethlehem and see this thing that has happened, which the Lord has made known to us" (Luke 2:15). Mary, with so many plates to balance (her betrothal to Joseph, her daily laundry list of chores she had never known before, taking care of her first baby and doing so on a shoestring budget), paused and "[pondered] these things in her heart" (Luke 2:19).

Preparing to address a gathering of real-estate professionals, I phoned two friends who are Realtors and asked what topics they would want to hear a speaker address in a similar setting. Each replied almost immediately, "Whatever you talk about, include a look at stress." Each then elaborated, using very comparable words (occasionally, the exact same phrases), about how that particular moment in history was a great season for Realtors. Houses were selling like hotcakes. Frequently, an offer was made, and in five days there was a closing. But each referred to the same specific downside of that. One of them put it this way: "It isn't a matter of not succeeding. Instead, it's a matter of being so busy that you don't have time to enjoy your success."

We sometimes push ourselves past the breaking point with a thousand things, never pausing to observe, to really see and to ponder the main thing that is right before us. We are so busy that we don't get to enjoy our successes, so hurried that we fail to

---

1. Stephen Covey, *The 7 Habits of Highly Effective People: Powerful Lessons in Personal Change*, qtd. in Goldberg, "Keep the Main Thing," para. 4.

appreciate or nurture our relationships. Or, in the race and rush of December, we are too stressed to even enjoy the meaning of Christmas. It's like sitting in a Manhattan restaurant but never really seeing New York because we're occupied with our cell phones. I wonder sometimes in my own life: What lesser things are keeping me from really seeing, enjoying, and understanding the main things?

Our current age almost screams out at us to rethink our priorities, our ways of relating to others, and the spiritual commands of primary commitments in life. It implores us simply to notice the beauties and blessings that surround us virtually all the time. If ever there were a season for interrupting a thousand busy things with a commitment to silence, to personal meditation, to prayer, and (as with Mary) to "pondering" the deeper meanings of life, Advent is that time. Otherwise, amid the busyness of things, even the busyness of the Christmas season, we miss the quiet majesty that is right before us. We come to the holiday but miss the birth. And ultimately, we go away from December feeling just as stressed, just as frustrated, just as tired, and just as empty as we felt before.

Part of the wisdom of the wise men, the shepherds, and young Mary was that they were able to step away from the countless demands regularly placed upon them and seek and see and ponder. For a while, they focused on the one single thing that mattered most of all: "Where is he who has been born king of the Jews?" (Matt 2:2).

18

CREDITS

Matthew's Gospel begins with a passage most of us skip over, a lengthy genealogy that preceded the birth of Jesus: "The book of the genealogy of Jesus Christ, the son of David, the son of Abraham. Abraham was the father of Isaac, and Isaac the father of Jacob, and Jacob . . ." (Matt 1:1–2). On and on it goes for forty-two generations until at last he writes, "And Jacob [obviously a very different Jacob than the one mentioned in verse 2] the father of Joseph the husband of Mary, of whom Jesus was born, who is called Christ" (Matt 1:16). The genealogy extends from Abraham to Jesus, the two key names of the whole Judeo-Christian history.

For those who do read that long list, most of the names included are far less familiar than Abraham's or Jesus'. They are names of people that, aside from biblical scholars, time has all but forgotten: "And Rehobo'am the father of Abi'jah, and Abi'jah the father of Asa, and Asa the father of Jehosh'aphat, and Jehosh'aphat the father of Joram, and Joram the father of Uzzi'ah, and Uzzi'ah the father of Jotham, and Jotham the father of Ahaz, and Ahaz the father of Hezeki'ah . . ." (Matt 1:7–9). Who were those folks? What good things did they accomplish in life? What bad deeds were they guilty of? Again, unless one is a serious student of Jewish biblical history, who knows much, if anything at all, about Abi'jah, Uzzi'ah, or Ahaz? What legacy belongs to those almost-anonymous individuals in Matthew's list of forty-two generations? This is their shared legacy: They were ancestors of Abraham and predecessors of Jesus. They served, at least, the purposes of keeping one story alive and preparing the way for the next story to be told. Theoretically, had any of them failed to honor his or her role in the story, Jesus might not have been born at all.

At the close of every movie, while the theme song is being played or sung one last time, there is a list of credits that scrolls down the screen. They include the names of the cast members, producers, and the director, but also other names: casting directors, colorists, fashion designers, visual-effects artists, unit production managers, wardrobe assistants, camera workers and grips, transportation attendants, caterers, etc. Unless the theme song is compelling, most folks do not stay to read the Matthean-like "genealogy" of those whose work went before the showing of the film. Their names remain anonymous except to a very few. And yet, were it not for what each of them does, the rest of us would never be able to see Bradley and Jennifer kiss in the closing scene or Bond emerge alive and victorious over the latest threat to global security. The unheralded contributions of persons whose names are not long remembered make possible the movies and the stars and the Golden Globes and Oscars that follow.

In Matthew, we are reminded that the ultimate star of the show is Jesus. The message *is* the Messiah. But that gospel also includes a loud "hooray" for Salathiel and Eliakim and their unnamed spouses, for women and men whose life stories are unknown with one exception: they did what was needed to prepare the way for the one who was to come. Their names are part of the credits that roll at the end of the sacred movie, without which the movie could have been a very different tale to tell.

Matthew's genealogy teaches us that *little things count*, that seemingly small contributions can have exceedingly large and important impacts. A friend sent me an internet article written by a man who helps construct airplanes. The author noted that when we think of the people who make up that industry, immediately pilots and airline attendants and maybe even ticket agents come to mind. He, on the other hand, works eight hours a day in a factory making aircraft fairings. Until reading his story, I had never even heard the term "aircraft fairings." He explained that aircraft fairings are the things attached to the wings of airplanes that help them bend without falling off. Something most of us would agree about is that when flying in a plane, we would prefer that the wings do not fall off! "The next time you exit an airplane and thank the captain," he wrote, "say a word of thanks for me, too—the guy without captains' wings who made sure the plane's wings stayed on tight."

Little things count. Unnoticed deeds by unnamed people keep the planes of life functional. Acclaim does not always denote value any more than anonymity denotes the lack of it. Josiah Gilbert Holland wrote:

> Heaven is not reached at a single bound;
> But we build the ladder by which we rise
> From the lowly earth to the vaulted skies,
> And we mount to its summit round by round.[1]

Our contributions to the overall worth of life—to kindness, charity, and common humanity; to making goodness, decency, integrity, and compassion priorities; to setting quiet examples of positivity and hope; to making a dent in the ethos of anger with expressions of forgiveness and love—are bricks that help build a better, stronger world whether or not our names appear on life's marquee. It's not about fame. It's about consistently doing what we can where we can when we can to prepare the way for goodness to prevail. Little things count, and in God's way of viewing life, they are not "little" at all.

A truth as sure as any is that we are called to keep doing the jobs that prepare the way for the one who comes, whatever those jobs may be. Mother Theresa's observation that we are not called to be "successful" but rather to be "faithful" is equally valid if we substitute other words for "successful," words like "famous,"

---

1. Holland, "Gradatim," ll. 29–32.

"applauded," or "celebrated."[2] And so we offer thanks to every Abia, Ozias, or Achaz; to every butcher, baker, candlestick maker, or builder of aircraft fairings who does their best to honor the one who comes at Christmas and to make life better for others. Learning from their examples inspires us to become part of that sacred genealogy so that even if our names only appear on the closing credits, we will have done something that added worth to the story.

2. "I was not asked to have success, but to have faith" (Mother Teresa, qtd. in Yesudas, "Like Mother Teresa," para. 1).

19

INNKEEPERS

The Gospel writers did their own unique things in their own unique ways to serve their own unique senses of calling.

Mark wrote with a sense of urgency based on Roman persecutions and with a sense of expectation due to his belief in the imminent return of Jesus. When we know his audience and their context, we begin to comprehend why Mark doesn't even include a birth story. He isn't as concerned with how Jesus got here as with how he believed Jesus would get here again in the near future.

John's primarily Greek audience was enthralled by philosophy and the intellectual search for truth. They were not interested in sweet or sentimental stories about shepherds and mangers. Knowing that, we understand why John wove his birth narrative around the theology of incarnation: "The Word [the very mind of God enlightening us in our search for truth] became flesh and dwelt among us" (John 1:14).

When we identify Matthew as a Jewish Christian author writing to a Jewish audience about a Jewish Messiah, then we understand why he uses so much Moses language and imagery in telling the Jesus story, and why Joseph, a descendant of Abraham and David, takes center stage over Mary in his birth narrative.

Then there is Luke, who was more of an outlier, a Roman writing to a gentile audience who also felt like outliers. Luke traveled with Paul, the great evangelist to the gentiles, and thus predictably wrote a Gospel focusing on inclusivity, on how all people (not just a select few) are important. In his other book, the Acts of the Apostles, Luke continued that theme from start to finish—the theme of how Jesus isn't just interested in *us* but also loves and came for and died for *them*, and how any time we hold groups of people at arm's length because they are different from us, we then distance ourselves not just from them but also from Jesus (no matter how loudly we may talk about believing in and loving him).

The Christmas story from Luke's Gospel challenges us to determine whether or not we have allowed ourselves to become innkeepers (people who shut other people out): "And she gave birth to her first-born son and wrapped him in swaddling cloths, and laid him in a manger, because there was no place for them in the inn" (Luke 2:7). Luke confronts us about who we choose to turn away, who we decide not to invite into the inn of our lives, our friendship circles, our compassion, and even our churches.

Dina Donohue wrote a classic Christmas story entitled "Trouble at the Inn." It is about a nine-year-old child named Wally Purling, a second grader who should have been in fourth grade. He had been held back because he lacked sufficient academic abilities to progress as other children did. Wally was a large, gentle boy with cognitive-development challenges. December came, and it was time for the annual Christmas pageant. Each year, the second graders performed the traditional birth story from Luke's Gospel. Miss Lumbard, the second-grade teacher, was faced with a conundrum. Every child had to have a role in the play. But what would she do with Wally? He wasn't able to learn many lines. His nine-year-old size made him stand out from the other seven-year-old children. And yet, no child could be left out of the performance. At last, Miss Lumbard had an idea. She would cast Wally as the innkeeper. His size would make him seem imposing when he turned Mary and Joseph away. And he would only have two lines: "What do you want?" and (when Joseph asked for lodging) "Seek it elsewhere! The inn is filled." Surely, with enough rehearsing, Wally could do that much.

The day of the play arrived. Parents, grandparents, teachers, and other students gathered in the auditorium to watch. Initially, all went according to plan. Then came the moment the teacher had worried about, the moment when Mary and Joseph arrived at the inn. Would Wally be able to remember his lines?

He opened the door to the inn and asked, just as they had rehearsed numerous times: "What do you want?"

Joseph replied, according to the script: "We seek lodging."

Wally answered: "Seek it elsewhere. The inn is filled."

Miss Lumbard breathed a sigh of relief. To her pleasant surprise, Wally had learned his lines and played his part correctly. Sadly, Joseph placed an arm around Mary's shoulder and turned away to walk into the dark of night. They had taken only a few steps when the audience heard a voice break script. It was Wally. With a smile on his face, he cried out: "Don't go, Joseph. Bring Mary back. You can have my room."[1]

Luke tells the story of the innkeeper because his readers knew what it felt like to be turned away. As gentiles (and especially as Romans following the fall of Jerusalem in 70 CE), they had been judged and shut out by the religious leaders of Israel. Luke's audience understood how it felt to be pushed aside, to be banished to the second tiers and balconies and dark alleys of life. Therefore, he knew they would be drawn to the story of a Messiah who understood how overlooked or dismissed they felt because he, too, had been treated like an outsider—shut out, pushed aside, banished. Luke said to his readers that Jesus would never close the door on them but that he always made room in his life for those the world had judged or rejected. Thus did Luke encourage his readers to do for others what Jesus had done for them—to be inclusive, open-hearted, and transformed into the likeness of a second-grade child who made room for those whom others would push away.

Luke is all about tearing down walls and building bridges in their places. He reminds us that Jesus was born for the people we resent, against whom we are biased, whom we would reject or even hate, whom we avoid when we see them walking down the hall, as

1. Donohue, "Trouble at the Inn."

much as he was for us. And not only was Jesus born for them as much as for us, but he also died for them as much as for us. And he calls all people to diminish the word "them" and to nurture the word "us." In short, to read the Christmas story from Luke challenges every Christian to ask, "Have I allowed myself to become an innkeeper? And if so, do I have the moral courage to instead be transformed into the likeness of a child named Wally?"

20

ADVENT AND REPENTANCE
(Thoughts about Justice and Mercy)

A fourth-grade Sunday school teacher was instructing her children about the doctrine of repentance. As part of the lesson, she had each student say a prayer out loud that began with the statement "Lord, make me a better boy or a better girl," followed by an idea of how they might become that: "Lord, make me a better girl so I will stop getting mad at my little brother." "Lord, make me a better boy so I will quit looking at the test paper of the girl who sits beside me in math class." On and on they went until finally, they reached that one child every class has. Apparently, he either misunderstood or simply didn't much care for the idea of repentance. So he prayed, "Lord, I don't want to be a burden to you. So, you can just make all the other kids better, because I'm pretty happy the way I am."

In Advent, there are certain words that command our attention, words like "prepare," "pray," "peace," and a host of others. One such word which Advent brings into decided focus is "repent." John the Baptist began his preaching about the arrival of Jesus with the statement "*Repent*, for the kingdom of heaven is at hand . . . Prepare the way of the Lord, make his paths straight. . . . I baptize you with water for *repentance*, but he who is coming after me is mightier than I, whose sandals I am not worthy to carry; he will baptize you with the Holy Spirit and with fire" (Matt 3:2–3, 11, italics added). In a manner worthy of any fiery evangelist, John challenged: "Repent, for the kingdom of heaven is at hand!"

In the original Greek, the word "repent" actually means "to turn in a new direction."[1] It's not a scary word. It's a smart word. It's a word about sometimes getting off course in life and needing to redirect ourselves in order to find what we need to find or arrive where we need to go.

Repent. Reset your GPS. Take a new road. Follow a different pathway. If ever there is a perfect time for doing that, it's during Advent when we begin to seriously think about what really matters, when we begin to tinker with priorities, and when we begin to pray like most of those Sunday school children, "Lord, make me a better boy or girl, a better man or woman. Help me to find a better way to live. Help me to turn in a new direction."

The prophet Micah reminded his listeners of two directions in which we need to turn, two roads we need to travel in order to find life: "What does the LORD require of you but to do justice, and to love kindness, and to walk humbly with your God?" (Mic 6:8). Walking humbly with our God is the faith part. Justice and mercy are the roads Micah says we have to travel in order to get there.

First of all, says the prophet, from time to time we need to turn in the direction of *justice*. There are two kinds of justice. One is a universal experience, a divinely ordered sense of right and wrong in the universe. Over the course of time, the scales of life do inevitably balance.

When people get to know my wife and me as a couple, they no doubt wonder (and sometimes are bold enough to say out loud), "How on earth did you get her?" I have a ready answer. I tell them that somewhere in the distant past, maybe I did something awfully good, and she is my reward for that. And somewhere in the distant past, maybe she did something so regrettable that I am her punishment. The scales of life balance.

All joking aside, we have seen how that principle does, in fact, happen. Plant seeds of anger or arrogance, and you reap loneliness. Plant love or kindness, and you reap friendships. That is what Jesus

---

1. Floyd, "New Shoots," para. 28.

was talking about when he said, "So the last will be first, and the first last" (Matt 20:16). The scales of life balance. There is a universal sense of justice.

But justice is not merely universal. It is also existential. In that sense, justice is very particular and very personal. In short, I am called to be an agent of justice in the here and now. "What does the LORD require of you but to do justice, and to love kindness, and to walk humbly with your God?" (Mic 6:8). To *do* justice—to help make it happen in your world. And that's where repentance comes in. Too often I stop with merely complaining about injustice. To turn in a new direction means that I move from complaining about the problem to contributing to a solution.

Name your issue, from human rights to environmental concerns, from helping those who cannot help themselves to helping create a climate of kindness, from addressing trafficking to addressing loneliness, from making the world safer for children to making the world less overwhelming for their great-grandparents. Turning in a new direction involves not merely lamenting the way things are but also standing up and speaking out about the way things ought to be. That's what's required to become agents of justice in a sometimes unjust world.

Micah also advised that we are called to perform acts of *mercy*. "What does the LORD require of you but to do justice, and to love kindness, and to walk humbly with your God?" (Mic 6:8).

A few Decembers ago, a photo appeared on the front page of the *New York Post*. It showed a manger scene in front of a church in Brooklyn. Apparently, a number of feral cats had decided to nest there at night, finding the straw in the manger to be a warm place to make their beds. The headline above the photo said, "Strays in the Manger." Most of us from time to time have been able to identify with that caption. We know how it feels to be left out or left behind, unnoticed or unwanted, like a stray in a cold, lonely world. Life teaches, however, that almost always when we are trapped in the nighttime of our journey, someone comes to our manger (a friend, a family member, a church member, or even a stranger).

Someone comes who does something or says something to turn the lights on in the darkness.

Isn't that how Jesus himself comes to us most of the time—through humans who, knowingly or not, offer his mercy when we need it most? Returning to my church office after lunch on an unseasonably mild December day, I came face-to-face with four young people on Fifth Avenue in front of Starbucks. They were carrying signs that said, "Free hugs." One of them looked at me and asked, "Do you want to hug? It's free." Being an introvert by nature, I just smiled, shook my head, and said, "No thanks. Seriously, thanks, but no," and kept walking. Later, I wished I had said yes to them. Later still, I wished that I could become like them. You and I cannot fix the whole world, but we can be a moment of mercy for individuals here or there who need mercy, who feel like strays in the manger and desire simply to find a bit of shelter from the cold night of life. Sometimes that's what "repent" means. It means no longer simply standing on the sidelines, looking at people and hoping or even praying for the best for them. It means turning in a new direction and extending kindness, compassion, and mercy.

"Repent," said John, and get ready for the arrival of the Messiah. Take a new pathway. Turn in a new direction. Micah joined in by saying, "Those directions will lead you to justice and mercy." When we reset our spiritual GPS in those directions, we will be ready for the Messiah when he comes.

21

HOST AND HOSTESS GIFTS

Ordinarily, it is customary to take a gift when invited to someone's home. It doesn't have to be extravagant. Sometimes folks regift something they received and don't plan to use. In the Christmas season, there are probably unopened boxes of fruitcake that have been circulating since Charles Dickens was a boy. The point is that we thank the people who have invited us into their homes by giving them a token of our gratitude. We called them "host and hostess gifts."

Usually, this tradition works out nicely. Once in a while, however, not so much. Over the years, I've been given lovely gifts, but I also (and I'm not exaggerating) have been given Chia pets and Soap on a Rope. Martin Marty, the former editor of *Christian Century* and one of the most wonderful people I have had the privilege of meeting (a man who is a brilliant theologian, writer, and preacher), was invited to a housewarming in Chicago for a young couple who had just moved into their new home. On the written invitation, it was stated that the couple had all the essentials they really needed and thus would prefer that housewarming gifts take the form of gags. They invited everyone to find "the tackiest, ugliest gift imaginable" and promised that at the party there would be an award given to the person who brought the ugliest gift of all. Marty said it took a long time to open the gifts that evening. Many were, in fact, little short of hideous. As they were about to unwrap a present brought by one of their coworkers, the bearer of the gift said, "Of all the ugly things that you have been given tonight, I promise you mine is the worst. I diligently searched all over Chicago to find a gag gift that would make you gag, and this is it. You might as well go ahead and give me the award as tonight's winner before you even open the box." Then the couple opened it to find a huge yellow ceramic bird that was a hanging planter. It was, in Marty's words, "the ugliest-shaped bird you have ever seen, with a color even uglier—not quite yellow and not quite orange and not even close to attractive." He said he was surprised when there was a very minimal, almost nervous chuckle, and then the couple laid the man's gift aside and hurriedly moved on to unwrap another. It was obvious the giver's feelings were a bit hurt by the fact that they didn't laugh uproariously as he had expected they would. Later in the evening, Marty discovered the reason for the couple's subdued response to the man's "ugly gift." When he walked into their kitchen, Marty spotted above their sink, dangling from a chain, the exact same yellow-bird hanging planter with a cactus plant inside. It was something the couple had bought intentionally and hung in their house because they thought it was attractive. Sometimes the gifts we bring (or that others bring to us) don't work out as we had hoped.

Such is never the case with the one for whom we wait in Advent. When he comes, the gifts he brings are unique and transformational.

In Ps 126, the psalmist reflects on the hard times Israel had suffered, especially the years of captivity and oppression. There were years of slavery in Egypt and Babylon. They were held against their wills. They were battered emotionally. They were afraid they would never see their homeland again. The psalmist compares them to "he that goes forth weeping, bearing the seed for sowing" (Ps 126:6). And they sowed those seeds with tears (Ps 126:5). But then something happened. Someone came to their door with a gift no one else could give—the gift of liberation from their captors, of freedom and the chance to return home. And so the psalmist says,

"We were like those who dream. Then our mouth was filled with laughter, and our tongue with shouts of joy" (Ps 126:1–2).

Luke includes verses we call the Magnificat, that wonderful song of praise young Mary sang when an angel appeared and told her she would give birth to the Messiah. There she was, a teenaged girl from Nazareth (an obscure little village with just a handful of mostly poor working families). Mary was likely a child of poverty, possessing a future without many possibilities and with lots of problems, including the very real likelihood of working hard and dying young. But suddenly, an angel told Mary a guest was coming, one for whom Israel had waited and prayed for centuries. Moreover, that guest was coming to her. Mary responded in song: "My soul magnifies the Lord . . . for he has regarded the low estate of his handmaiden. . . . He who is mighty has done great things for me" (Luke 1:46–49).

Each of those Scripture lessons tells of people who had nothing but tough luck and hard times until a guest arrived with the power to change their stories. And so, new endings are written that would not have been imaginable before: "Our mouth was filled with laughter, and our tongue with shouts of joy" (Ps 126:1–2). "He who is mighty has done great things for me" (Luke 1:49). That is Advent's promise. A December guest will come, bringing with him a host or hostess gift that no one and nothing else can offer.

What gifts does this Messiah bring to our doors, to our lives?

First of all, he brings *a sense of purpose*. A personal friend who is a physician told me about a study he read that explored factors that contribute to longevity. A large group of people who had reached the age of one hundred or more was studied to determine what accounted for their extended years. Though we might have expected the word "genetics" to be at the top of the list, it was not. Because of factors like medication and nutrition, nowadays if we know the genetic road signs to watch for, we can avoid many potential problems. Two of the top-three components that produce longer lives, predictably, were exercise and diet. My friend said that the third item on the list, however, surprised him. The study said a major contributing factor to longevity is possessing a sense of purpose. Those who get out of bed every morning with something they feel they need to do or something of value to contribute to the world apparently live demonstrably longer lives. Certainly, whatever the length of one's mortal journey, living with a sense of purpose results in what Jesus called "life abundant" (John 10:10).

A retired minister I knew many years ago spent his entire career serving tiny, out-of-the way little churches on hillsides in the Appalachian Mountains. He never got his name in the news. He never made much of a salary. He loved his children, but they had to work their own ways through college because he didn't have enough money to send them. Still, they adored him because they knew he loved and did the best he could for them. His church members adored him, too, because they knew the same thing. He was there for them in their good times and their terrible times. His was neither an easy nor an affluent life. He and his family lived in parsonages with wood-burning stoves for heat and strategically placed buckets when it rained to catch the water that came through the ceiling. As an old man confined to a wheelchair in a nursing home for those of limited income, he said to me, "It's been a great life. I wish I could do it all over again!"

Making the Christian journey one where we love, serve, befriend the lonely, listen, forgive, encourage, lift the fallen, and heal the wounded provides us with what that mountain minister found—life that is "abundant" and filled with purpose and meaning, life that makes you want to get out of bed in the morning and at the end causes you to say, "I wish I could do it all over again!" That's what this December guest brings to us, a kind of life that makes us say with Mary: "He that is mighty has done great things unto me!"

What does the Messiah bring as gifts for hosts and hostesses when he knocks on their doors? He brings a sense of purpose . . . and also *a sense of peace.* "And his name will be called 'Wonderful Counselor, Mighty God, Everlasting Father, Prince of Peace'" (Isa 9:6). And the angels sang, "On earth peace among men . . ." (Luke 2:14). He brings a peace "which passes all understanding" (Phil 4:7).

Years ago, I heard a preacher tell the story of a woman named Mary Williams, who was for years a nurse in a large university hospital and who received a thank-you note from a man whose wife had died. Ms. Williams was her nurse, tenderly caring for her until the woman's last breath was drawn. She also dealt gently and compassionately with the husband and the couple's six-year-old little boy. In the thank-you note, the widowed father wrote:

> I want you to know what my son said to me the morning after his mother died. He said, "Daddy, it was easier letting Mommy go to heaven to live with God last night because God sent Jesus to be with us at the hospital." Ms. Williams, my son was talking about you. You were Jesus to him, and probably to me as well. In our worst moment, God sent you to us, and you were our source of peace.

In life's most trying moments, God sends Christ to us. Sometimes it is through the mystery of his Spirit. Sometimes it is through the presence of other believers. But he comes and brings the gift of "peace that passes understanding" (Phil 4:6).

What does the December guest bring as a host or hostess gift to those who open the door? He brings *a sense of purpose* that makes "life abundant" and *a sense of peace* that brings light even amid the darkness. Those are the gifts that, once received, cause us to sing out with Mary, "He who is mighty has done great things for me" (Luke 1:49).

22

THE SERENADE FOR SHEPHERDS[1]

I read that a man in Wisconsin "broke a Guinness World Record" for having gone to a theater to watch the movie *Captain Marvel* 116 times.[2] I'm not sure any of us can (or would ever want to) match that, but how many times have you seen your favorite movie? For me, it's *Field of Dreams*. I must have watched it a half dozen times and would see it again tonight if it were on. Every time, even though I know it's coming, I still tear up at the end when Ray says to his father, "Dad, want to have a game of catch?" My wife's favorite is *A Chorus Line*. Between the movie and the stage play, I'm sure she's seen it at least a dozen times. She loves the music, she loves the dance, and she loves the story of people who persevere because of their love for their art. I've heard some folks say that, given their frequency on television, they have seen *The Wizard of Oz* or *The Sound of Music* twenty times or more. I have a friend, an actor in New York City, who went to see *Fences* with Denzel Washington and Octavia Spencer and was so blown away by it that he remained and watched it a second time that day. Then, within the next six days, he went back four times more. He saw the

1. "The Serenade for Shepherds" was originally a sermon preached on ABC TV on Christmas weekend, 2021, as a presentation of The Interfaith Broadcasting Commission and sponsored and hosted by High Point University.

2. "Wisconsin Man Breaks Record."

movie six times in one week because he was so overwhelmed by the acting. How many of us every December curl up on the sofa beneath our favorite blanket with a bowl of popcorn on the table and watch *It's a Wonderful Life* or *A Christmas Carol* yet again? And yet again, we get misty when Clarence receives his wings or Scrooge at last gives Bob Cratchit a raise.

Frederick Beuchner says that one of the reasons why stories are so powerful is that at some point, we know it isn't just a story about characters on the screen or the page. It is also a story "about us."[3] That is why the story of the shepherds still keeps our attention even when we hear it for the umpteenth time. It's about a group of minimum-wage employees working the third shift outside Bethlehem in the dark and cold of night, unseen and forgotten by all those other townsfolk "nestled all snug in their beds; / While visions of sugar-plums danced in their heads."[4] Not so for the shepherds on a hill in the darkness, worried that every nighttime noise was a wolf coming to attack the sheep or, perhaps, to attack the shepherds. Each time that story is read, no matter how many times we've heard it, we lean forward a little because something down deep inside us whispers, "That story's not just about shepherds. It's about us—especially the part that says, 'And they were filled with fear' (Luke 2:9)."

> Who are the shepherds?
> They are the hungry, the poor,
> With empty pantries and rotting floors.
> They are innocent children made to cry
> By abusive adults on whom they rely.
> They are the victims of bias, hatred, or fear.
> They are people with sickness hovering near.
> They are successful adults but tormented inside
> By guilt or emptiness they manage to hide.
> They are lonely women, forgotten men,
> Or those with regrets for what could have been.
> They have well-rehearsed smiles and wipe away tears
> Lest anyone notice if they should draw near.

3. Buechner, "Power of Stories," para. 3.
4. Moore, "Visit from St. Nicholas," ll. 5–6.

Who are the shepherds? Who might they be?
The shepherds are you. The shepherds are me.[5]

Most of us know about being shepherds, don't we? We know
about what Thomas Moore called "the dark nights of the soul"[6]
or what Luke said it feels like to be "filled with fear" (Luke 2:9).
From time to time, all of us shepherds fear that a wolf may appear on the horizon, and we give that wolf a variety of names:
illness, injury, grief, guilt, cancer, COVID-19, estrangement,
aging, loss, loneliness. The midnight hour on a hill outside
Bethlehem can be a frightening place.

The truth is, of course, that fear itself is often the most dangerous wolf of all. We've all read the statistics that say about 85
percent of the things we worry about never occur.[7] That means
that we allow ourselves to be immobilized by imagination.

A six-year-old boy offered to help his mom after dinner.
She was busy tidying up. Dad had returned to the office for a
meeting. It had snowed that day, so Mom took her son's offer,
handed him a broom, and said, "Please go outside and sweep
the snow off the steps so it will be safe tomorrow morning."

The little boy answered, "Mom, it's dark out there. I'm
afraid of the dark."

She said, "Son, it's just the other side of this door. I'm right
here, not five feet away. There's nothing to be scared of. Now go
sweep the steps."

"No, Mom," he argued. "I can't. I'm afraid of the dark. I
can't see what's out there."

His mother looked at him and replied, "Son, there is nothing to be afraid of. Jesus will be in the darkness with you."

He was quiet for a moment, thinking about her words.
Then he cracked the door just slightly, stuck the broom through,
and said, "Jesus, since you're out there anyway . . ."

5. Poem by the author.

6. See Moore, *Dark Nights*.

7. Pawlowski, "How to Worry Better," para. 13.

The mother was correct. Much of the time, there is far less to fear than we imagine.

Most of the things we fear never occur. A student approached me during the first week of a semester and said, "I'm afraid I'm going to fail this class."

I answered, "You've been in class for two days. Two days! You haven't had time to become afraid yet." If he was that nervous in my Introduction to the New Testament class, I wondered how freaked out he must be when entering Physics! I advised him, "Don't let your semester be defined by fear." To his credit, the young man hung in there. As I recall, he made a B or a B+, a good grade. The point is this: Do not allow your future to be defined by fear.

Most of the things we fear never occur. But sometimes, some do. Sometimes life can be hard at midnight near Bethlehem.

I made that statement to seven hundred people in an auditorium for a Christmas service. They looked like they had it together. They were so "put together," so nice and on top of things. "But," I said to them, "who knows what emotions you are wearing on your faces beneath the COVID-19 masks? Who knows what heavy burdens you are carrying on your shoulders right now that no one else can see?" We were filming that night, and I knew that whatever states of affairs may have existed for those within the auditorium, beyond that beautiful space, people from all across America would watch not only from their houses but also from hospital rooms and hospice centers and homeless shelters. Or they would be alone in their apartments in New York or Nashville, Detroit or Dallas, Louisville or Los Angeles, or any of a thousand other places, perhaps just having returned from a divorce court or a funeral parlor. A few years ago after preaching a televised Christmas Eve service, I received a letter from a man on the other side of the country. He said, "I write to you from my prison cell. Your church looked so beautiful on TV. It made me remember Christmases when I was a boy, going to church with my mom and dad. If only I could turn back the clock."

We know what it's like to be shepherds. But it was shepherds in the darkness who heard a serenade from angels: "Be not afraid; for behold, I bring you good news of a great joy . . . For to you is born this day in the City of David [or Chicago or Cincinnati or Atlanta or Albuquerque or wherever you are] a Savior, who is Christ the Lord" (Luke 2:10–11). "For to you" personally, on your own private hillside in your own private midnight hour, comes the "good news of a great joy" that, as that mom told her son when she handed him the broom, "Jesus will be in the darkness with you."

Every time I teach a New Testament class, I introduce my students to the Greek word *paraclete*. It's an impressive-sounding word. I always tell the students to go home during fall, Christmas, or spring break and casually drop that word in a conversation with their parents. I promise my students that later that night, their parents will say to one another, "Did you hear that? Junior is speaking Greek. Missy knows the Bible. Every penny we've forked over in tuition is paying off!" *Paraclete*. It's the Greek New Testament word for the Holy Spirit. Its common definition is "One who walks alongside." "Behold, I bring you good news of a great joy" as you face whatever dark night of the soul you may be going through (Luke 2:10). "For to you is born this day in the city of David a Savior" who, when he became an adult, made a promise: "Lo, I am with you always" (Luke 2:11, Matt 28:20). "To you is born this day" someone who will walk alongside you on every road, at every step, in every moment and every situation, every day, everywhere. Fred Craddock put it well in a sermon: "Initially when we learn of Jesus, we hope that wherever Christ is, there is no misery. But in time as we journey with him and observe all his encounters with those who suffered, we learn that wherever there is misery, there Christ is."[8]

On a warm Saturday night in July, I went to bed feeling like a million bucks. Three hours later, I woke up feeling like I had been hit by a truck (that then backed up and ran over me again). Despite being vaccinated, I was one of the minority who still contracted a breakthrough case of COVID-19. Thankfully, the vaccination kept

8. Craddock, "Jesus Saves."

me out of the hospital or worse, but still, being sick wasn't exactly a walk in the park. Three days in, I was sent to a nearby hospital for an infusion of monoclonal antibodies. The infusion center had three recliners, each with a post beside it where the IV infusion bag was hanging. In the recliner next to mine was a woman who appeared to be somewhat advanced in years. In all likelihood, she was probably thinking of me similarly, "The old guy must be sick!" She was kind, wore a smile, and was genuinely polite to the young nurse who ran some risks to provide good medical care for us. You could tell just by observing that the woman beside me was a gentle spirit. Over the course of the hour and a half we were there, the nurse regularly checked on us to make sure all was okay. At one point, the woman in the recliner next to mine rather casually said to the nurse, "I had to cancel my appointment with the oncologist in order to come here."

I thought, "Oh my gosh! Not only does she have COVID-19, she has cancer as well."

Apparently, the nurse was concerned by that remark, and asked, "Do you live alone?"

The woman answered, "Yes, physically I do live alone. But I know someone is there with me."

With that, just as casually as before, she went back to reading her book. She was a shepherd on a midnight hill with two serious wolves howling in the distance. But she was not afraid, because she had heard the serenade of angels: "Be not afraid; for behold, I bring you good news of a great joy . . . for to you is born this day in the city of David a Savior, . . . [and he] will be with you always [to walk alongside you every day, on every road, at every step] (Luke 2:10–11).

Who are the shepherds? We are. I don't always know what dark nights of the soul others may be enduring. I wish I had a magic wand to wave and make it all go away, but there is no such thing. There is, however, a promise that whatever your life is like right now, for better or worse, a choir of angels is singing you a serenade: "For to you is born this day in the city of David a Savior, who is Christ the Lord" (Luke 2:11). For to you *personally* is born someone who will walk alongside you, someone to lean on, to talk to, someone who is in your corner, whose arms gently wrap around you to hold you close and to hold you up. "For to you is born this day in the city of David a Savior, who is Christ the Lord." That, as I understand it, is "good news of a great joy."

23

REJOICE!

A number of years ago, I heard a woman tell of the aftermath of a serious automobile accident she suffered. Following the accident, she spent two full months in a body cast. She's fine now, but she spoke of the day in a hospital rehab unit when she was anything but fine. As she began to heal, the injured nerves were waking up and screaming at her about the decision she made one night to take a shortcut and drive on a dark, curvy back road in the rain to save twenty minutes. Her still-strained muscles and mending bones had joined the chorus. It was 20 degrees outside but felt like a 110 inside a body cast in an all-too-well-heated room. She was sweating. She was itching, but couldn't reach inside the cast to scratch. "I was utterly miserable," she reported.

At that moment, her mother walked into the room to visit. She looked distracted, troubled. The daughter asked from her rehab bed, "Mom, are you okay?"

Her mother lifted her index finger and answered, "Not really. Look at this. I did it a few minutes ago while sealing an envelope. There's nothing in the world worse than a paper cut!"

The woman telling the story noted, "I guess life is a matter of perspective."

Consider the story of Mary. No, not that Mary but a different one. I came to know her many years ago while serving as a student pastor at a rural church a few miles from the campus of Duke Divinity School. Mary was confined to bed due to several different illnesses, each debilitating. She was poor and lived in a small and old mobile home at the end of a dirt road at the edge of the woods. She and a cousin shared that space, though the cousin was away eight to ten hours a day, five days a week, cleaning houses. Their provisions were meager. Whereas some dine on salmon or steak, Mary and her cousin ate a lot of souse meat (a sausage-like concoction in appearance made of the parts of hogs that are ordinarily swept up and thrown away following slaughter) donated by a nearby farmer. Clothing came from Salvation Army or Goodwill stores.

On weekends as a student pastor, I visited church members who were homebound or hospitalized. So, from time to time I sat by Mary's bed, shared news with her from an outside world she never saw anymore, listened to her memories, and concluded each visit with a prayer. In Mary's room was a small skylight window. Through it, she could catch just a glimpse of the sky overhead. She would often say, "When it's dark, I look up until I fall asleep. I can see stars glittering, and if it's positioned just right in the sky, I can even see the moon winking goodnight. Through that window, I see a little corner of heaven. And that reminds me how beautiful the rest of it must be."

"Rejoice!" sang those first-Christmas angels from their corner of heaven. Their words were heard by shepherds working late on a hill outside Bethlehem, taking care of someone else's property, overworked and underpaid, almost unnoticed by the world, probably poor, often discouraged, maybe lonely. "Rejoice!" sang the angels, helping the shepherds and the rest of us understand that joy is almost never the result of what we have in life but rather how we look at life. Something wells up within us when we catch just a glimpse of a corner of heaven, even amid the ordinariness or pains of our existence?

There is, of course, the other Mary—the one an angel called "favored one." "You have found favor with God," the heavenly messenger proclaimed (Luke 1:28, 30). You can almost hear her answer, "Me, favored? Seriously?" She, also poor, young (probably in her early teens), and unprepared for the message she received, could not at first comprehend the angel's words: "Behold, you will conceive in your womb and bear a son." "How shall this be," she answered, "since I have no husband?" (Luke 1:31, 34). She would be shamed and shunned and, possibly, even stoned back home in Nazareth. "Not trying to be impertinent, Mr. Angel, but is that what you consider 'favored'?" The angel continued, "He that is conceived in you is of the Holy Spirit. And you shall call his name Jesus, for he will save all people from their brokenness" (paraphrased from Luke 1:31–35). Mary had seen a little glimpse of heaven. Did she fully understand? Of course not. Could she theologically interpret? That's highly unlikely. But having seen the glimpse she was given, Mary answered, "Behold, I am the handmaid of the Lord; let it be to me according to your word . . . My soul magnifies the Lord, and my spirit rejoices in God my Savior . . . for he who is mighty has done great things for me" (Luke 1:38, 46–47, 49).

To catch a glimpse of the heavenly nature of things and thus to rejoice almost never has anything to do with winning the lottery or a political office or the Super Bowl. It happens in simpler, softer, subtler moments when we least expect it . . . sometimes even in moments when we struggle or suffer or stumble in the dark. And suddenly, unexpectedly, in the midst of all that we hear an angel's voice.

On a Pentecost weekend several years ago, Rev. Becca Stevens (founder of Thistle Farms ministry in Nashville) brought some of her graduates to our church in New York to lead an educational retreat about the ministry of Thistle Farms. They were women who had been trafficked, beaten, and literally "owned" by wicked men. Many had been involuntarily drugged until they became addicted and thus had lengthy records with law enforcement. One by one they had been forced into prostitution. They had every reason to be bitter and resentful, but the amazing work done at Thistle Farms had liberated them from painful pasts and given them new chances at productive and peace-filled futures. At lunch following worship, one of those women remarked to my wife and me, "This has been such a great weekend. Isn't life beautiful? Every day reminds me of how good God is." I don't remember her name, but it should have been Mary. "My soul . . . rejoices in God my Savior . . . for he who is mighty has done great things for me" (Luke 1:46–47, 49).

I spend too much time lamenting paper cuts while others celebrate a glimpse of heaven through a tiny overhead window. I wander through the season of Advent feeling more stress than anything else while another who has defensible reasons for negative emotions says, "Every day reminds me of how good God is."

In God's way of doing business, maybe the rule is not "Whoever has the most, wins." Maybe instead the rule is "Whoever catches a glimpse of heaven—whoever recognizes blessings in the midst of pain and hopefully somehow passes those blessings along to others—will understand the meaning of the word 'rejoice'!"

24

DID YOU GET EVERYTHING
YOU WANTED?

I grew up in a neighborhood where seven of us, all roughly the same age, lived in four houses next door to each other and one directly across the street. Every Christmas Day, we had a routine. Following lunch, we would gather together for our version of a tour of homes, journeying from house to house examining what each one of us had received that morning. At every stop along the tour, there was a predictable litany of questions:

- "Did you put it together, or did your parents do it?" (If we had put the toy together, there was a sense of accomplishment. We were able to imagine our dad at 2:00 a.m. giving up and blurting out loudly, while our mom tried to calm him, "Never again will I purchase anything in a box that has the words 'Some assembly required'!" It was a sign of victory if it took our know-how to make the toy work.)

- "Does it require batteries?" (If something had to be plugged in, you could only use it in a prescribed place. But if it used batteries, the toy was mobile, and thus limitless vistas came into view.)

- "Can I try it?" (It was new, after all. So this question basically meant, "Do you trust me?")

- And there was one question you could pretty much count on whichever house we were in. At some point, just two of us kids would be together and would ask in hushed tones so that the parents couldn't possibly hear (we did possess at least a little sensitivity): "Did you get everything you wanted?"

"Did you get everything you wanted?" I have reached the point in life where I don't care whether or not an item requires batteries. And if some assembly is required, I don't even want it. But that last question is still a good one: "Did you get everything you wanted for Christmas?"

Had anyone asked that question of Mary, how do you think she would have answered? Clearly, she got a lot she had not bargained for. In her early teens, she was little more than a child rearing a child. Shortly after the birth, she became a newlywed. In fact, when she became pregnant, Mary was only "betrothed" (legally committed to Joseph but without the religious ceremony). Soon, she became an immigrant in Egypt in order to protect her baby against Herod. She was poor. The only cradle she had for her child was an oxen's feeding trough. She found herself having to balance the responsibilities of marriage and parenting at an age when most of our granddaughters are trying out for the middle-school cheerleading squad.

"Did you get everything you wanted?" How would Mary have answered? At the close of his telling of the Christmas story, Luke says, "But Mary kept all these things, pondering them in her heart" (Luke 2:19). Whatever else she may have lacked, whatever other challenges she may have faced, Mary knew that a miracle of indescribable magnitude had occurred. She had been given something that mattered more than anything else in all the world, the sacred gift of God's Son, who was also her son. "Did you get everything you wanted, Mary?"

And she answers, "I got more than I could ever have hoped for or dreamed of. I was given Jesus. I, of all people, experienced Christmas."

"Did you get everything you wanted?" you ask Simeon or Anna. They are old—a prophet and a prophetess who went to the temple every day for decades, hoping against hope that maybe that was the day the long-awaited Messiah would show up. For centuries, the primary prayer of the Hebrew people had been that God's anointed Deliverer would come. They had been oppressed and threatened, occupied or taken captive. There was Egypt, the Amalekites, the Syrians, the Assyrians, the Philistines, the Babylonians, and now the Romans. "How long, O LORD? Wilt thou forget me for ever? How long wilt thou hide thy face from me? How long must I bear pain in my soul?" (Ps 13:1–2). But suddenly, one day in the temple before their plaintive prayer could be spoken, it was answered. Joseph and Mary entered with their newborn child.

"Simeon, Anna, did you get everything you wanted?"

And the old, wise ones would reply, "We received what we have wanted all our lives. We received what Israel has wanted for generations. We received a person, *the* person, whose coming we have awaited with prayers and tears for centuries." At last, the aged prophet was able to say, "For mine eyes have seen thy salvation" (Luke 2:30).

Ordinarily, I think, that's how Christmas happens. It comes to us through the gift of people. Wrapped presents are dear and almost always sincerely appreciated, but in essence, they are simply reminders of the love of the people who gave them to us. It is in the presence of people that the divine presence is most powerfully experienced.

Some time ago on a Sunday night, I began to ponder in my heart what I suspect were some self-indulgent and negative things. I began considering some of what we lose as we age—some of the things we can't do that we once took for granted and some of the roles we played that others are now playing in our place. Thinking those thoughts left me not merely nostalgic but also sad. The feeling of sadness remained with me all day Monday. On Monday night, however, my melancholy was interrupted. That night, we went to our older daughter's house for our grandson's second birthday party. It was half organized chaos and half unfettered joy, exactly what birthday parties for two-year-olds are supposed to be. My five-year-old granddaughter's voice was a constant: "Poppa, look at this! Poppa, watch me do that!" Meanwhile, our grandson was visibly excited about every toy, especially a Tonka earthmover that he could ride on. Chocolate cake was served, and little arms wrapped around my neck, leaving tiny chocolate fingerprints behind.

Over the course of that week, I received a number of unanticipated contacts from friends of many years. There was a Zoom call from a longtime friend in Florida. He said, "We haven't talked in a year. It's time to catch up. And just hearing your voice isn't enough. I want to see your face again." The very next day, I heard from another long-standing friend who said, "When can we get together between now and Christmas?" Before the week was over, two other colleagues did the same, each suggesting a meal together to celebrate the holidays. One is a man I have known for over half a century. He closed our conversation with the same words he has used to close every conversation since we were teens: "Love you, brother!" Added to all that were Christmas cards from acquaintances, emails from students, gifts from people who had sat for many years in my congregations, and unexpected gestures of love from family members. By the end of the week, the mist of the preceding Sunday had vanished away in the warm sunlight of people. And that is what I kept and pondered in my heart as did Mary, Simeon, and Anna. Christmas is about people, which is what the Bible says Christmas has always been about. "And the Word became flesh and dwelt among us" (John 1:14).

An indisputable truth about life is that we can be as poor as Jim and Della in O. Henry's story "The Gift of the Magi," but if we have one another, we are rich.[1] What more life-enhancing gift can we receive than individuals whose goodness and grace, whose smiles and softness, are reflections of that other person who came at Christmas long ago and continues arriving for us if we pay attention? "For to you is born this day . . . a Savior," and everyone who makes life beautiful and bright is a reflection of that person.

"Mary, did you get everything you wanted for Christmas?"

---

1. Henry, "Gift of the Magi."

"I got all that and more," she answers. "I got more than I could ever have dreamed of receiving. It came in a person 'wrapped in swaddling cloths.'" And for the rest of her life, she "kept all these things, pondering them in her heart" (Luke 2:19).

25

O HOLY NIGHT

Feeling nostalgic prior to my final Christmas Eve service after a decade as pastor of Marble Collegiate Church, I remarked to a friend, "This beautiful experience will be over for me after tonight. I won't get to do Christmas Eve services again."

He (a good theologian and purebred realist) answered, "Will there still be Christmas Eves?"

"Yes," I replied.

"Will you still go to church?"

"Of course," I answered.

"Will there still be people of faith gathered there? Will they still read the story from Luke chapter 2? Will there still be music? Will the snow still fall?"

"You know all that will happen," I told him.

"So, Michael," he said, "is Christmas Eve about all that, or is it just about you?"

My friend's was a great and sobering and helpful observation, one that I needed to hear. It put things back into a proper perspective for me. Though the Christmas story applies to each of us in deeply personal and even intimate ways, it ultimately is about more than just us. It's about some things that are unchanging and have been around for two thousand years. It's about magic ("And suddenly there was with the angel a multitude of the heavenly host" [Luke 2:13]); about surprise ("For to you is born this day in the city of David a Savior" [Luke 2:11]); about God's presence in places where we didn't expect God to show up ("And she gave birth to her first-born son . . . and laid him in a manger" [Luke 2:7]); about "peace [on earth] among men with whom he is pleased!" even in a world where peace seems like little more than a foolish pipe dream (Luke 2:14). Christmas is about the positive, unchanging things that bring light out of darkness, hope out of despair, courage out of fear, laughter out of weeping, and life out of death. For two thousand years, our world has been hearing that unchanging and life-changing message. For all the millennia yet to come, that same message will be heard: "Behold, I bring you good news of a great joy which will come to all the people; for to you is born this day in the city of David a Savior, who is Christ the Lord" (Luke 2:10–11).

A few years ago, a young soldier from Wisconsin spent Christmas in Afghanistan. He said he was used to Christmases that were cold, with evergreen trees bent low under the weight of snow waiting on his dad's ax and his mother's act of making the tree glow with lights and garlands. He was used to family, hearty laughter, and holiday meals with those he loved. "But that Christmas," he said, "there was none of that. No snow. Just a hot desert outpost. No tree. Just scrawny shrubs here and there. No lights. Just cut-out paper decorations taped to those scrawny limbs. They served turkey in the mess hall, but it couldn't hold a candle to the ones my mom would bake and place on the table alongside her yams and cheeses and pumpkin pie." It was a disappointing, lonely day.

The young man reported:

> That evening, the chaplain set up an altar in the mess hall. Some of us gathered there and listened as he read the story of Joseph, Mary, and a baby born in a place just as desolate as the one we were in. When he read the words "Unto you is born this day . . . a Savior," suddenly I felt my spirit lift. It dawned on me that the same Jesus who was present in Bethlehem and in Wisconsin could

be just as present in the desert of Afghanistan. I began
to sense that Christmas really is about more than snow
and trees and pumpkin pie. Instead, Christmas is about
the one who comes in the snow or in the desert, in the
church or in the mess tent, in a home or in a manger. As
long as we remember that, then we discover "good news
of great joy" wherever we are.

His insight was theologically and personally accurate and
faithful. Christmas isn't just about us, our wants, our needs, our
wishes. It is instead about the one who comes.

That being noted, in another sense, Christmas actually is
about us—at least about how Jesus' arrival intersects our lives.
"For to you is born this day in the city of David a Savior . . . !"
(Luke 2:11). For to *you*! And unlike Santa, it really doesn't matter
whether you or I have been naughty or nice. Jesus cares as much
about the naughty children as the nice ones, as much about the
broken as the beautiful, as much about the lonely as the loved, as
much about the forgotten as the famous, as much about the sinner
as the saint, as much about those who think they don't need him
as about those who know they do. In fact, sometimes his passion
appears even a bit deeper for those who exist in life's mangers. He
said, "Those who are well have no need of a physician, but those
who are sick" (Matt 9:12).

It's not about me. It is about me. Which is true? The answer
is very much like my response to my wife's traditional inquiry
when dessert is offered following holiday meals. She always provides more than one choice. She goes around the table asking each
person one by one, "Do you want the chocolate chess pie or the
pound cake with ice cream?" When she comes to me, it's with sort
of a smile and sort of a grimace because she knows my answer
is going to be Yes. It's not an either-or thing to me. Instead, it's
both/and. Is Christmas about the one who comes with salvation
to impart? Absolutely and unequivocally, it is. Is Christmas about
those of us who desperately need what only he can bring? Just as
absolutely and unequivocally, it is. Is it about him or about us? And
the answer is Yes.

BIBLIOGRAPHY

Breathnach, Sarah Ban. *The Simple Abundance Journal of Gratitude*. New York: Warner, 1996.

Buechner, Frederick. "The Power of Stories." *Writing for Your Life* (blog). https://writingforyourlife.com/the-power-of-stories-by-frederick-buechner/.

Craddock, Fred. "Jesus Saves." Filmed July 10, 2011, in Nashville, TN, at Woodmont Christian Church. YouTube, 22:21. https://www.youtube.com/watch?v=OobgXCEtmes.

Dickens, Charles. *A Christmas Carol*. New York: Foresman & Co., 1920.

Donohue, Dina. "Trouble at the Inn." October 27, 2014. https://www.guideposts.org/inspiration/people-helping-people/trouble-at-the-inn.

"Francis of Assisi: A Period of Crisis—Embracing the Leper." *Friarmusings* (blog), November 9, 2012. https://friarmusings.com/2012/11/09/francis-of-assisi-a-period-of-crisis-embracing-the-leper/.

Goldberg, Efrem. "Keep the Main Thing the Main Thing." August 29, 2021. https://aish.com/keep-the-main-thing-the-main-thing/.

Henry, O. "The Gift of the Magi." In *The Complete Works of O. Henry: The Definitive Collection of America's Master of the Short Story*, 7–11. Garden City, NY: Doubleday, 1953.

Holland, Josiah Gilbert. "Gradatim." https://sharpgiving.com/101famouspoems/poems/original/082Holland.html.

King, Martin Luther, Jr. "Remaining Awake through a Great Revolution." March 31, 1968. https://seemeonline.com/history/mlk-jr-awake.htm.

Moore, Clement Clarke. "A Visit from St. Nicholas." https://www.poetryfoundation.org/poems/43171/a-visit-from-st-nicholas.

Moore, Thomas. *The Dark Nights of the Soul*. New York: Piatkus, 2011.

Nothwehr, Dawn. "The Franciscan View of the Human Person: Some Central Elements." https://www.franciscantradition.org/images/stories/custodians/13_Nothwehr_FINALnew1.6.17.pdf.

Parris, James. "Why Was Edward VIII's Abdication a Necessity?" https://www.thehistorypress.co.uk/articles/why-was-edward-viii-s-abdication-a-necessity/.

Pawlowski, A. "How to Worry Better." NBC News, December 13, 2017. https://www.nbcnews.com/better/pop-culture/praise-worry-why-fretting-can-be-good-you-ncna757016.

Reed, Lawrence W. "The Love of Power vs. the Power of Love." *Freeman: Ideas on Liberty* (May 2007) 14–15. https://fee.org/articles/the-love-of-power-vs-the-power-of-love/.

Rheins, Jason. "Plato's Allegory of the Cave: Part I." February 25, 2022. https://montessorium.com/blog/plato-s-allegory-of-the-cave-part-i.

Schaefer, Linda. "Mother Teresa: A Woman of Faith." https://www.osvnews.com/amp/2021/08/23/mother-teresa-a-woman-of-faith/.

Thurman, Howard. "The Work of Christmas." December 2009. https://www.bread.org/sites/default/files/downloads/howard-thurman.pdf.

Tourgee, Heather. "How the Puritans Banned Christmas: In 1659 the Puritans Banned Christmas in Massachusetts. But Why?" December 8, 2021. https://newengland.com/today/living/new-england-history/how-the-puritans-banned-christmas/.

Van der Kiste, John. "King Edward VIII and Mrs Simpson." https://www.thehistorypress.co.uk/articles/king-edward-viii-and-mrs-simpson/.

"Wisconsin Man Breaks Record by Watching 'Captain Marvel' 116 Times." NPR, April 19, 2019. https://www.npr.org/2019/04/19/715053876/wisconsin-man-breaks-record-by-watching-captain-marvel-116-times?t=1657609017161.

Yesudas, Fratel. "Like Mother Teresa, We Are Not Social Workers, but Co-workers in the Love of God." AsiaNews, November 12, 2009. https://www.asianews.it/news-en/Like-Mother-Teresa,-we-are-not-social-workers,-but-co-workers-in-the-love-of-God-16842.html.